20 Lesson Frameworks *for* Elementary Grades

Teaching COMMON CORE English Language Arts Standards

Patricia M. CUNNINGHAM
James W. CUNNINGHAM

Solution Tree | Press
a division of
Solution Tree

555 North Morton Street
Bloomington, IN 47404
800.733.6786 (toll free) / 812.336.7700
FAX: 812.336.7790
email: info@solution-tree.com
solution-tree.com

Printed in the United States of America

18 17 16 15 14   1 2 3 4 5

Library of Congress Cataloging-in-Publication Data

Cunningham, Patricia Marr.

  Teaching common core English language arts standards : 20 lesson frameworks for elementary grades / Patricia M. Cunningham, James W. Cunningham.

    pages cm

  Includes bibliographical references and index.

  ISBN 978-1-936763-25-2 (perfect bound) 1. Language arts (Elementary)--Curricula--United States--States. 2. Language arts (Elementary)--Standards--United States--States. I. Title.

  LB1576.C858 2015

  372.6--dc23

            2014021711

Solution Tree
Jeffrey C. Jones, CEO
Edmund M. Ackerman, President

Solution Tree Press
President: Douglas M. Rife
Editorial Director: Lesley Bolton
Managing Production Editor: Caroline Weiss
Developmental Editor: Sarah Payne-Mills
Copy Editor: Rachel Rosolina
Text and Cover Designer: Laura Kagemann

Acknowledgments

Solution Tree Press would like to thank the following reviewers:

Tabetha Finchum
Fourth-Grade Teacher
Centennial Elementary School
Tucson, Arizona

Jane Ching Fung
First-Grade Teacher
Alexander Science Center School
Los Angeles, California

Brandi Leggett
Third-Grade Teacher
Prairie Ridge Elementary School
Shawnee, Kansas

Beth Maloney
Fifth-Grade Teacher
Sunset Hills Elementary School
Surprise, Arizona

Susan Carpenter O'Brien
Fifth-Grade Teacher
Weatherbee School
Hampden, Maine

Pam Reilly
Second-Grade Teacher
Woodbury Elementary School
Sandwich, Illinois

Table of Contents

About the Authors vii

Introduction 1

Chapter 1   Guess Yes or No 11

Chapter 2   Find It or Figure It Out 21

Chapter 3   Question It 27

Chapter 4   Gist 33

Chapter 5   Themes, Morals, and Lessons Learned 41

Chapter 6   Main Idea Tree 53

Chapter 7   Sequence / Cause and Effect 63

Chapter 8   Compare and Contrast 73

Chapter 9   Text Features Scavenger Hunt 85

Chapter 10   Preview-Predict-Confirm 97

Chapter 11   Point of View 105

Chapter 12   Poetry Aloud 121

Chapter 13   Plays Aloud 129

Chapter 14   Word Detectives 135

Chapter 15   Ten Important Words .141

Chapter 16   Be Your Own Editor 147

Chapter 17   What's Your Opinion? .155

Chapter 18   Teach Me 163

Chapter 19   Tell Me a Story 171

Chapter 20   You're the Expert! 181

References and Resources 191

Index 193

About the Authors

 **Patricia M. Cunningham, PhD,** is a professor of education at Wake Forest University in North Carolina. She has been an elementary school teacher, a reading specialist, and director of reading for a county school system.

Dr. Cunningham specializes in finding alternative ways to help struggling readers. She is author of *Phonics They Use, What Really Matters in Spelling, What Really Matters in Writing,* and *What Really Matters in Vocabulary.* She is coauthor of *Classrooms That Work* and *Schools That Work.*

She earned a master's degree in reading from Florida State University and a doctorate in reading from the University of Georgia.

 **James W. Cunningham, PhD,** is a professor emeritus of literacy studies at the University of North Carolina at Chapel Hill. He has taught at the elementary and secondary levels and served as a consultant with schools, districts, and other education agencies in twenty-five states.

Dr. Cunningham has written books, book chapters, research articles, professional articles, and scholarly reviews. He has spoken at many U.S. and international conferences. He was a member of the Text Complexity Committee for the Common Core State Standards for English language arts. He is a member of the Reading Hall of Fame.

He earned a master's degree and doctorate in reading education from the University of Georgia.

To book Patricia M. Cunningham or James W. Cunningham for professional development, contact pd@solution-tree.com.

Introduction

There are not enough hours in a day or days in a school year to teach the Common Core State Standards for English language arts (CCSS ELA) one at a time. And there is no reason to! The idea underlying this book is that many of these standards relate to and complement each other, and teachers can develop them simultaneously. An integrated lesson in which students gather information through listening or reading and communicate with each other by speaking or writing can help you work toward several of these goals at the same time, or as Pat's mother would have put it, "Kill two (or more) birds with one stone!"

A Plethora of Standards

You may be familiar with the standards you are expected to teach in your grade. However, in many schools, teachers are less familiar with the standards in other grades. If the task of implementing the CCSS ELA feels overwhelming to you and your fellow elementary teachers, there are over 250 good reasons for that. Yes, there are thirty-two anchor standards and 250 grade-specific standards—250 standards that kindergarten through fifth-grade teachers are expected to implement and teach to their students (National Governors Association Center for Best Practices [NGA] & Council of Chief State School Officers [CCSSO], 2010). Skeptical about the mathematics? Table I.1 presents the breakdown.

Table I.1: K–5 CCSS ELA

Standards	K	Grade 1	Grade 2	Grade 3	Grade 4	Grade 5
Reading Literature*	9	9	9	9	9	9
Reading Informational Text	10	10	10	10	10	10

Continued →

Standards	K	Grade 1	Grade 2	Grade 3	Grade 4	Grade 5
Reading Foundational Skills	4	4	2	2	2	2
Writing	7	7	7	9	10	10
Speaking and Listening	6	6	6	6	6	6
Language	5	5	6	6	6	6
Total	41	41	40	42	43	43

* There is no literature standard for Reading standard eight (RL.8; see NGA & CCSSO, 2010, pp. 11–12).

Actually, even this count may underestimate the challenge. Yes, a second-grade teacher has forty separate English language arts standards to teach and assess this year. However, many of these standards have multiple goals! For example, Language standard four (L.2.4) requires second graders to:

> Determine or clarify the meaning of unknown and multiple-meaning words and phrases based on grade 2 reading and content, choosing flexibly from an array of strategies.
>
> a. Use sentence-level context as a clue to the meaning of a word or phrase.
>
> b. Determine the meaning of the new word formed when a known prefix is added to a known word (e.g., *happy/unhappy, tell/retell*).
>
> c. Use a known root word as a clue to the meaning of an unknown word with the same root (e.g., *addition, additional*).
>
> d. Use knowledge of the meaning of individual words to predict the meaning of compound words (e.g., *birdhouse, lighthouse, housefly; bookshelf, notebook, bookmark*).
>
> e. Use glossaries and beginning dictionaries, both print and digital, to determine or clarify the meaning of words and phrases. (NGA & CCSSO, 2010, p. 27)

Teachers have to teach these strategies to second graders. So, is Language standard four (L.2.4) one standard, or is it actually six?

A fifth-grade teacher has forty-three separate standards to teach and assess this year, and many of these standards also have multiple goals. For instance, Writing standard two (W.5.2) requires fifth graders to:

> Write informative/explanatory texts to examine a topic and convey ideas and information clearly.
>
> a. Introduce a topic clearly, provide a general observation and focus, and group related information logically; include formatting (e.g., headings), illustrations, and multimedia when useful to aiding comprehension.
>
> b. Develop the topic with facts, definitions, concrete details, quotations, or other information and examples related to the topic.
>
> c. Link ideas within and across categories of information using words, phrases, and clauses (e.g., *in contrast, especially*).

    d. Use precise language and domain-specific vocabulary to inform about or explain the topic.

    e. Provide a concluding statement or section related to the information or explanation presented. (NGA & CCSSO, 2010, p. 20)

If you teach second grade, there are sixty goals included in the forty standards. If you teach fifth grade, that number is eighty-five. Teachers of other grades are in a similar predicament. This analysis also assumes your students have all mastered the goals set for the previous grades. Is that a reasonable assumption? What about the struggling students in every school? What about the students who transfer into your school each year from somewhere else? Shouldn't you expect to reteach or review at least a few of the standards from previous grades? How can you possibly teach this huge number of capabilities in a way that all your students will learn them?

Moreover, in order to teach the CCSS, you must understand the special terminology and dot notation used to distinguish them: *strands, anchor standards, domains, grade-specific standards,* and *grade bands.*

- **Strands** are the four main divisions for the standards: (1) Reading, (2) Writing, (3) Speaking and Listening, and (4) Language. The Reading strand has two parts: Reading Standards for Literature (RL) and Reading Standards for Informational Text (RI). Foundational Skills (RF) are a third part specific to grades K–5 (see NGA & CCSSO, 2010b, pp. 15–17).

- **Anchor standards** define general, cross-disciplinary expectations for college and career readiness (CCRA). The anchor standards are numbered consecutively for each strand. For example, CCSS ELA-Literacy.CCRA.R.1 signifies college and career readiness anchor standard (CCRA), Reading strand (R), and anchor standard one (1). In this book, we use a simplified version of the standard designation—CCRA.R.1.

- **Domains** define categories of anchor standards for each of the strands. The domains are consistent across the grades and ensure continuity as the standards increase in rigor and complexity. The four domains in the Writing strand are (1) Text Types and Purposes, (2) Production and Distribution of Writing, (3) Research to Build and Present Knowledge, and (4) Range of Writing (see NGA & CCSSO, 2010, p. 18).

- **Grade-specific standards** define what students should understand and be able to do at the end of the year. These standards correspond to anchor standards with the same number designation. For example, RL.5.1 represents Reading Standards for Literature (RL), fifth grade (5), and standard one (1) in the domain Key Ideas and Details. Similarly, SL.3.1 represents Speaking and Listening (SL), third grade (3), and standard one (1) in the domain Comprehension and Collaboration. Additionally, we refer to standards that are applicable to all grades K–5 by the strand and standard number. For example, *Reading for literature standard one,* or just RL.1, and *Language standard five,* or just L.5, represent grades K–5.

- **Grade levels and grade bands** are groupings of standards by grade—*grade levels* for K–8 and *grade bands* for 9–10 and 11–12.

Implementing, teaching, and talking about these standards are hearty tasks for elementary teachers! No wonder many teachers feel overwhelmed. In this book, we hope to make this task less daunting.

Three Main Goals of the Standards

In our work with teachers, we have found it helpful to explain that, even though all the English language arts standards are important and must be taught, the three main goals of teaching these standards are to (1) improve students' reading comprehension, (2) improve their writing, and (3) promote independent reading and writing.

Reading Comprehension

First, think about the ten Reading standards. The first nine require reading comprehension of one sort or another. The tenth Reading standard, however, says that students will be able to meet the first nine standards in grade-appropriate texts. The Foundational Skills within the Reading standards exist so that students will have the decoding ability, sight words, and fluency necessary to comprehend the texts they read. Such skills are also covered in the other strands. For instance, Language standard five (L.5) includes the knowledge of figurative language important for comprehending grade-appropriate texts (see NGA & CCSSO, 2010, pp. 27–29). Language standards four and six (L.4 and L.6) focus on meaning vocabulary knowledge, long known to be essential for reading comprehension (see NGA & CCSSO, 2010, pp. 27–29). Of course, the Speaking and Listening standards are valuable in their own right, but Speaking and Listening standard one (SL.1) also includes student interaction and discussion, which play a facilitative role during comprehension instruction (see NGA & CCSSO, 2010, pp. 23–24). In addition, Speaking and Listening standards two and three (SL.2 and SL.3) include being able to comprehend while listening in ways parallel to Reading standards one, two, six, seven, and eight (R.1–2 and R.6–8; see NGA & CCSSO, 2010, pp. 11–14, 23–24). Similarly, Writing standards seven through nine (W.7–9) require students to comprehend literature and informational texts well enough to write about them (see NGA & CCSSO, 2010, pp. 19–21).

Table I.2 presents the number of standards that focus on reading comprehension.

Table I.2: K–5 CCSS ELA for Reading Comprehension

Standards	K	Grade 1	Grade 2	Grade 3	Grade 4	Grade 5
Reading Literature*	9	9	9	9	9	9
Reading Informational Text	10	10	10	10	10	10
Reading Foundational Skills	4	4	4	2	2	2
Writing	2	2	2	2	3	3
Speaking and Listening	3	3	3	3	3	3
Language	3	3	3	3	3	3
Total	31	31	31	29	30	30

* *There is no literature standard for Reading standard eight (RL.8; see NGA & CCSSO, 2010, pp. 11–12).*

By our calculation, improving students' reading comprehension is a goal of 182 of the 250 ELA standards—more than two-thirds of them!

Since reading comprehension is a goal of so many of the standards, it is important to understand what the CCSS mean by *reading comprehension*. Reading comprehension in the CCSS for grades kindergarten through fifth grade includes both close reading and higher-level thinking about texts. For instance, Reading standard one (R.1) focuses on close reading and is a prerequisite to all other Reading standards. Inferential comprehension is not a separate standard in the CCSS but is required for every Reading standard. Reading standard two (R.2) focuses on main idea comprehension. Reading standard four (R.4) requires students to learn word meanings during text comprehension. Reading standard six (R.6) expects students to deduce or infer a character's or author's point of view. Reading standard eight (R.8) reflects critical reading. Students are expected to be able to compare, contrast, and synthesize two or more texts (Reading standard nine; R.9) or a text with media (Reading standard seven; R.7). Never before has there been such a full and rich view of comprehension reflected in reading standards (see NGA & CCSSO, 2010, pp. 11–14).

Most significantly, the Reading standards make a major distinction between comprehending literature (stories, dramas, or poems) and informational text (historical, scientific, or technical writings). Every K–5 Reading standard applies to informational text, and every Reading standard except eight (R.8) also applies to literature. An examination of Reading standards two through nine (R.2–9), however, reveals just how different comprehension is for the two kinds of text (see NGA & CCSSO, 2010, pp. 11–14).

The National Assessment of Educational Progress (NAEP), or the *Nation's Report Card*, has steadily increased its use of informational text in grades 4, 8, and 12 assessments (National Assessment Governing Board, 2008). To coincide with this growing emphasis on informational texts, the CCSS call for an even distribution of reading literature (50 percent) and informational text (50 percent) by third grade (Coleman & Pimental, 2012). The CCSS do not specify a split between literature and informational text for grades K–2. It seems prudent, however, to have primary students read enough informational text to prepare them for the 50 percent split they will encounter in third grade. Furthermore, in grades 6–12, the CCSS call for a shift to substantially more literary nonfiction reading and instruction (Coleman & Pimental, 2012). By twelfth grade, the CCSS call for a 30 percent literature and 70 percent informational text distribution (NGA & CCSSO, 2010). For this reason, we recommend a 70 percent literature and 30 percent informational text split for reading lessons in grades 1 and 2.

Writing

Another principal purpose for teaching the CCSS ELA is to improve student writing. There are ten Writing anchor standards, each specifying an aspect of writing competence. In addition, Language standards one and two (L.1 and L.2) address the traditional concerns of usage and mechanics in writing or speaking. Language standard three (L.2.3) expects second-grade writers to know the difference between formal and informal language. It also expects them to make effective and precise word choices. Language standards four and six (L.4 and L.6) address meaning vocabulary knowledge, which is crucial for academic writing. Language standard five (L.5) addresses figurative language, which is helpful to writers as well. Additionally, Speaking and Listening standards four and six (SL.4 and SL.6) support improvements in student writing, and Reading standards seven through nine (R.7, R.8, and R.9) focus on reading comprehension required for writing about texts and other sources.

Table I.3 presents the number of standards that focus on improving writing.

Table I.3: K–5 CCSS ELA for Improving Writing

Standards	K	Grade 1	Grade 2	Grade 3	Grade 4	Grade 5
Reading Literature	2	2	2	2	2	2
Reading Informational Text	3	3	3	3	3	3
Reading Foundational Skills	0	0	0	0	0	0
Writing	7	7	7	9	10	10
Speaking and Listening	2	2	2	2	2	2
Language	4	4	5	5	5	5
Total	18	18	19	21	22	22

Improving students' writing is a goal of 120 of the 250 English language arts standards—almost half of them!

Since writing is a goal of so many of the standards, it is important to understand what the CCSS mean by *writing*. Notably, the Writing standards include the overall objective of writing instruction: that students will be able to write well for their grade (Writing standard four; W.4). Equally important, the Writing standards tell us how students are expected to achieve that objective: by writing a variety of types and lengths of texts routinely across the school day and week (Writing standard ten; W.10) and by using the writing process to develop and strengthen some of what they write (Writing standard five; W.5). The Common Core specifies three general types of writing (opinion pieces, informational pieces, and narratives) that students are expected to learn how to do well (Writing standards one through three; W.1–3). Students are also required to learn how to use technology to write and publish (Writing standard six; W.6). In addition, students are expected to both write about what they read (Writing standard nine; W.9) and do research (Writing standards seven and eight; W.7 and W.8). Language standards one and two (L.1 and L.2) require students to write with correct language usage and writing mechanics (spelling, capitalization, and punctuation) as well. The level of writing instruction the CCSS call for is the most comprehensive and powerful we have ever seen.

Reading and Writing Independence

There are two essential literacy activities that students must be willing to do independently before they leave kindergarten: (1) recreational reading and (2) first-draft writing. At every grade level, teachers have the challenge of making sure they have books available that all their students can and will want to read independently. They also have the challenge of establishing an atmosphere in which all students are willing to take the risk of writing independently, even though they know they can't yet spell every word correctly or abide by every grade-appropriate usage, capitalization, or punctuation convention. It does students no favors to allow them to resist independent reading or writing. Students' willingness to engage in these two activities is foundational for literacy growth.

Once students are willing to read and write independently, teachers can use a variety of instructional tasks to help them improve. In reading, many of these are complex comprehension tasks. In writing, many of these are complex revision and editing tasks. A dilemma that all teachers face is how much support to give in order to help students improve their reading comprehension and writing.

Gradual Release of Responsibility Model of Instruction

Many educators suggest that instruction should follow a gradual release of responsibility model (Pearson & Gallagher, 1983; Wilhelm, 2001). Where appropriate, teachers begin by assuming all the responsibility, modeling and thinking aloud about what they want students to do. This step can be most easily understood as "I do, and you watch." Next, teachers invite students to join them in deciding how to perform the task. This step can be thought of as "I do, and you help." In the third step, students assume much of the responsibility by working together in small groups, and the teacher becomes the coach, providing guidance and redirection as needed. This stage can be thought of as "You do it together, and I help." During this stage, the teacher observes the interaction among the students and formatively assesses how individuals are progressing and what kind of further instruction they need. Finally, when the teacher sees that students understand the task, students complete a task on their own that shows they have moved from teacher dependence to independent application. This final stage is the point at which summative assessment eventually takes place and can be thought of as "You do, and I watch."

Essentially, the gradual release of responsibility model requires lots of teacher and peer modeling and support for the first several lessons. During subsequent lessons, however, you remove some of that support until students are ready to work through the lesson framework on their own. At that point, you'll be able to use a summative assessment to document whether each student has moved from teacher dependence to independence. This way of thinking about instruction is intuitively appealing because it describes the way many of us learned most of the complex routines we perform. How did you learn to bake? To play tennis? To master all the technology you need in a modern classroom? Chances are, you watched someone, helped, tried it out with some friends or your mentor nearby, and eventually could orchestrate this complex task on your own without even thinking about it.

Thus, within most of the lesson frameworks that make up this book, we employ the gradual release of responsibility model to help you teach your students how to perform the complex tasks of thinking deeply about texts as they read and conveying ideas clearly and convincingly as they write. The two lesson frameworks designed primarily to build fluency, Poetry Aloud and Plays Aloud, do not follow this model because they are intended primarily for developing oral reading skills.

Twenty Lesson Frameworks to Teach the Standards

Since 2010, when the standards first appeared, we have been working with teachers to develop, adapt, and tweak their lesson plans so they are working on multiple standards simultaneously. This book is a result of that collaboration. Each of the twenty chapters presents a lesson framework you can adapt to your students, curriculum, and grade level. Some of these include graphic organizers and anticipation guides you may already use. Others (like What's Your Opinion?) will provide a fresh approach to meeting the standards. Our hope is that by using a variety of these lesson frameworks, you can provide multifaceted learning opportunities in which your students talk, listen, read, and write to become more competent and confident English language users. As your students develop these critical communication skills, they will also be learning the knowledge and strategies necessary to achieve the worthy objectives delineated in the CCSS ELA.

Because improving reading comprehension and writing are two umbrella goals of the CCSS ELA, many of the twenty lesson frameworks teach at least one of the Reading standards or one of the Writing standards. In turn, helping students achieve these two goals serves the third goal of enabling them to read and write independently. Of course, as promised, every lesson framework also teaches more than one standard.

Think of these lesson frameworks as recipes. We both like to cook, and we generally follow recipes when we do. We have a friend who is both an excellent and a creative cook—she can just look in her cupboard and refrigerator, see what's there, and prepare something delicious that uses what she has. She doesn't usually measure and claims she rarely makes the exact dish twice. Why don't we cook like Sharon? Because if we did, the quality of our culinary life would noticeably decline! Whatever ability she has to create a new recipe on her feet and have it turn out well is a talent both of us lack. However, we are reasonably competent at choosing tasty and nutritious recipes, tweaking recipes after we have followed them carefully a time or two, and consistently getting good results with them from then on.

Certainly, there are teachers who can create successful lessons that neither they nor anyone else has seen before. We admire and sometimes envy them, but in our experience, they are very rare. Most good teachers we have known benefit from having effective lesson frameworks. They use their professional expertise and knowledge of their students and materials to plan, tweak, pace, and repeat lessons as necessary in order to maximize effectiveness. The lesson frameworks in this book can be seen as a set of recipes for teaching the CCSS ELA. As with culinary recipes, each framework exists because it does something the others do not. However, across all twenty, most of the standards are taught. In fact, the most important or challenging standards for reading comprehension and writing are taught in several lesson frameworks, because students benefit from repetition with variety.

Table I.4 outlines the twenty lesson frameworks (and chapters), as well as the college and career readiness anchor standards and grade-level standards that each addresses. (The grade-level standards are specifically for lesson frameworks focusing on Reading Standards for Literature and Reading Standards for Informational Text—RL and RI, respectively.)

How to Use This Book

Treat this book as you would a cookbook. Don't feel like you should start at the beginning and read to the end. Each chapter can stand alone. Scan the brief introduction

Table I.4: Twenty Lesson Frameworks and the CCSS

Lesson Framework	Standards					
Guess Yes or No	CCRA.R.1	RI.4	CCRA.SL.1	CCRA.L.4		
Find It or Figure It Out	CCRA.R.1	CCRA.SL.1	CCRA.L.6			
Question It	CCRA.R.1	CCRA.SL.1	CCRA.L.6			
Gist	CCRA.R.1	CCRA.R.2	CCRA.SL.1			
Themes, Morals, and Lessons	CCRA.R.1	CCRA.R.2	CCRA.R.3	CCRA.SL.1		
Main Idea Tree	RI.2	CCRA.W.2	CCRA.W.10	CCRA.SL.1		
Sequence / Cause and Effect	RI.3	CCRA.W.2	CCRA.SL.1			
Compare and Contrast	CCRA.R.9	RL.3	CCRA.W.2	CCRA.W.10	CCRA.SL.1	
Text Features Scavenger Hunt	RI.4	RI.5	RI.7	CCRA.SL.1	CCRA.L.4	
Preview-Predict-Confirm	RI.4	RI.7	CCRA.W.2	CCRA.W.10	CCRA.SL.1	CCRA.L.4
Point of View	CCRA.R.1	CCRA.R.6	RI.8	CCRA.W.1	CCRA.W.10	CCRA.SL.1
Poetry Aloud	CCRA.R.1	CCRA.R.4	RL.5	RF.4b	CCRA.L.4	CCRA.L.5
Plays Aloud	CCRA.R.1	CCRA.R.4	RL.5	RF.4b		
Word Detectives	RI.4	CCRA.SL1	CCRA.L.4	CCRA.L.5	CCRA.L.6	
Ten Important Words	RI.4	CCRA.W.2	CCRA.W.10	CCRA.SL.1	CCRA.L.4	
Be Your Own Editor	CCRA.W.5	CCRA.L.1	CCRA.L.2			
What's Your Opinion?	CCRA.W.1	CCRA.W.4	CCRA.W.5	CCRA.W.10		
Teach Me	CCRA.W.2	CCRA.W.4	CCRA.W.5	CCRA.W.10		
Tell Me a Story	CCRA.W.3	CCRA.W.4	CCRA.W.5	CCRA.W.10		
You're the Expert!	CCRA.R.7	RI.9	CCRA.W.7–9	CCRA.SL.1	CCRA.SL.4–6	CCRA.L.1

and feature box introducing the standards to each framework, and use table I.4 to find lesson frameworks that will teach something your students need right now.

Each chapter offers a sample lesson with tips to guide your instruction and ends with a section that breaks out the standards and explains how the lesson framework helps teach them to students. As noted, many lesson frameworks follow the phases of the gradual release of responsibility model: "I do, and you watch," "I do, and you help," and "You do it together, and I help." These chapters conclude with a focus on the final phase—"You do, and I watch"—by looking at implementing the lesson framework across the year.

When you have located frameworks your students need, consider how successful they will be with them and how much they will enjoy participating in the lessons. To build their confidence (and yours!), begin with the lesson frameworks you think students will enjoy most. Mark the others they need, which might be more difficult or less engaging, and plan to use them after success with the frameworks you deemed more engaging.

We wish you every success in teaching the CCSS to all your students!

CCSS in a Guess Yes or No Lesson

Guess Yes or No is a lesson framework you can apply to any informational text. When you lead students through this lesson several times and gradually release responsibility to them, you are helping them learn the reading, speaking and listening, and language skills in the following standards.

Reading

CCRA.R.1: Read closely to determine what the text says explicitly and to make logical inferences from it; cite specific textual evidence when writing or speaking to support conclusions drawn from the text.

RI.2.4: Determine the meaning of words and phrases in a text relevant to a *grade 2 topic or subject area.*

RI.3–5.4: Determine the meaning of general academic and domain-specific words and phrases in a text relevant to a *grade-level topic or subject area.*

Speaking and Listening

CCRA.SL.1: Prepare for and participate effectively in a range of conversations and collaborations with diverse partners, building on others' ideas and expressing their own clearly and persuasively.

Language

CCRA.L.4: Determine or clarify the meaning of unknown and multiple-meaning words and phrases by using context clues, analyzing meaningful word parts, and consulting general and specialized reference materials, as appropriate.

Source: Adapted from NGA & CCSSO, 2010, pp. 10, 13–14, 22, 25.

CHAPTER 1

Guess Yes or No

In 1978, Harold Herber, a pioneer in the field of content-area reading, proposed that teachers focus students' attention on key information in a text by presenting them with statements and having them guess which statements were true. Students then read the text, determined which of their guesses were correct, and turned false statements into true statements. Guess Yes or No is based on Herber's anticipation-guide strategy, a prereading tool to engage students and build new knowledge.

In Guess Yes or No lessons, students learn to read closely to determine whether statements are true or false, make logical inferences, and cite textual evidence to support their responses. Before students read the text, they read the statements together, and the teacher helps them use context and morphemic clues when appropriate to determine word meanings. Using the gradual release of responsibility model of instruction, Guess Yes or No combines student trios and teacher-led conversations to discuss various aspects of the text's content.

A Sample Guess Yes or No Lesson

Miss G.'s class is about to read an article on Japan from the student news magazine the class has a subscription to. She wants students to read the article closely and pay attention to the facts they learn about Japan. To plan the Guess Yes or No lesson, she reads the article and constructs a sheet with ten statements, some true and some false. (See figure 1.1, page 12.) She writes the false statements so that they can be turned into true statements by changing a word or two. In addition, she includes some statements that require students to make logical inferences to decide whether they are true or false. She also includes key vocabulary words students need to be able to pronounce and understand in order to fluently read the text.

Guess Yes or No: Japan

_____ 1.   Japan is on the continent of Europe.

_____ 2.   Mt. Fuji is a volcanic mountain in Japan.

_____ 3.   Japan has one of the lowest life expectancies in the world.

_____ 4.   The capital of Japan is Tokyo.

_____ 5.   Rice, fish, and seaweed are staples of the Japanese diet.

_____ 6.   Most people in Japan live in large houses out in the country.

_____ 7.   Japan is made up of thousands of islands in the Atlantic Ocean.

_____ 8.   Japan is the world's largest economy.

_____ 9.   Japan's national sport is Sumo wrestling.

_____ 10. Karaoke is a very popular recreational activity in Japan.

Figure 1.1: Sample Guess Yes or No sheet on Japan.

TIP

Try having your students work in trios—with a few duets or quartets—if your class doesn't divide equally by three. In many classrooms, if the group size is too large, some students spend time vying for control of the group, and other students just sit and let the bossy ones do the work!

This is the first Guess Yes or No lesson Miss G. has taught to her students. Miss G. follows the gradual release of responsibility model when teaching comprehension lessons. The class will watch and listen as she models how to figure out whether the first two statements are true or false. Students will help her figure out the next two as a class. Then, the students will work together in their trios to complete the final six statements. Miss G. has assigned students to trios so there is at least one good reader and one struggling reader in each trio.

Purpose Setting and Vocabulary Building

The lesson begins with Miss G. working with the whole class. The student assistant for the day hands out the Guess Yes or No: Japan sheet to everyone so each student has a copy.

Miss G. then sets the purpose for the lesson.

She says, "Today we are going to be learning about Japan. I have written ten statements here about Japan, but some of them are not true facts. Before you read, you are going to guess whether each statement is true or false. You are going to write your guesses in pencil so that you can change them based on what you read in the article. It doesn't matter how many you guess right before you read. What matters is that you can use your close-reading skills to figure out what the true facts are and change your guesses. Before we read, however, we need to read all ten statements together and make sure we know how to pronounce all the words and what they mean. Everyone read the first one with me."

The students all read the first sentence: "Japan is on the continent of Europe."

It is clear to Miss G. that some students don't know the words *continent* and *Europe* because their voices drop off at those words. *Continent* and *Europe* are two key vocabulary terms Miss G. intends to focus on.

Once the class reads the first statement, Miss G. asks vocabulary-building questions: "Who knows how many continents there are in the world? Can we name them all? What continent do we live on? Has anyone ever been to another continent?"

The students share their accumulated knowledge about continents, and then Miss G. asks them to write *yes* or *no* to show whether they think Japan is on the continent of Europe. Some students are hesitant to guess and protest that they don't know the answer. Miss G. assures them that they aren't supposed to know and that that is why the lesson is called Guess Yes or No. She waits until everyone has written *yes* or *no* on the line before going to the next sentence.

When everyone has guessed, the class reads the second sentence together: "Mt. Fuji is a volcanic mountain in Japan."

Again Miss G. asks vocabulary-building questions: "What is a volcanic mountain? Do we have any volcanic mountains nearby us?"

She writes the words *volcano* and *volcanic* on the board and asks if anyone has ever seen a volcano. She also helps students understand how *volcano* and *volcanic* are related, saying, "A volcanic mountain is a mountain that was formed by a volcano."

She then waits for everyone to write his or her guess before having students read the next sentence chorally: "Japan has one of the lowest life expectancies in the world."

Miss G. helps students determine the meaning of *life expectancy* and makes the morphemic connection with *expect*. She then asks them what they think the current life expectancy is for them and their parents. The students have varied answers, and this question clearly intrigues them. Miss G. tells them that since what they are going to read is about Japan, the article probably won't tell them about life expectancies in the United States. One student quickly interjects, "We can google it!"

The students write their *yes* or *no* guess, and everyone reads the next sentence chorally: "The capital of Japan is Tokyo."

Miss G. asks students what the capital of the United States is and what the capital of their state is. She explains that the capital is the place where government happens. She writes the words *capital* and *capitol* on the board and helps students distinguish between these words that sound alike but have different meanings.

Students record their guesses and read the next sentence together: "Rice, fish, and seaweed are staples of the Japanese diet."

Miss G. asks students to name some staples of their diet. Students express amazement that anyone might eat seaweed, but several students think Japanese people probably eat a lot of rice and fish. As they are making their guess, they want to know if all three have to be staples of the Japanese diet if they guess *yes*. She assures them that a *yes* guess has to include all three. It is clear from their response that they are eager to read the magazine article and see if Japanese people eat a lot of seaweed.

Before proceeding to the next sentence, Miss G. picks up the stapler from her desk and helps the students realize that they know another meaning for *staples*. One student chimes in that it can also be the store Staples.

The lesson continues as Miss G. leads the students to read each sentence chorally, builds meaning vocabulary, and has students guess *yes* or *no* for each of the remaining statements.

I Do, and You Watch

When the class has read all the statements, and Miss G. has developed all the key vocabulary, Miss G. asks students to gather in their assigned trios and hands the magazine to one student in each trio who quickly positions him- or herself in the middle between the other two students. Miss G. has learned that students work together and interact more when they have only one copy of the text to share. Even though she has enough copies of the magazine for everyone, students will only use one per trio for this lesson.

When the students are positioned in their trios, she has everyone turn to the page where the article begins and draws students' attention to the map at the beginning of the article. She models how to determine if the first statement is true by thinking aloud about the map and letting them listen in on her thinking.

She says, "Here is a map, and I find Japan here. I see that Japan is in Asia, so the first statement must be false. Japan is not on the continent of Europe. It is in Asia. I will change the first statement to make it true." (See figure 1.2.)

TIP

Have the less able reader hold the text and sit in the middle. This increases the chances that the student will be engaged, and holding the text confers status!

Guess Yes or No: Japan

_____ 1. Japan is on the continent of ~~Europe~~. *Asia*

_____ 2. Mt. Fuji is a volcanic mountain in Japan.

_____ 3. Japan has one of the lowest life expectancies in the world.

_____ 4. The capital of Japan is Tokyo.

_____ 5. Rice, fish, and seaweed are staples of the Japanese diet.

_____ 6. Most people in Japan live in large houses out in the country.

_____ 7. Japan is made up of thousands of islands in the Atlantic Ocean.

_____ 8. Japan is the world's largest economy.

_____ 9. Japan's national sport is Sumo wrestling.

_____ 10. Karaoke is a very popular recreational activity in Japan.

Figure 1.2: Sample Guess Yes or No sheet with revisions.

"Now, I will read this paragraph and see what I can find out about any of the other statements."

She reads the paragraph aloud and then explains her thinking. "This paragraph tells us that there are many volcanoes in Japan, and that Mt. Fuji is the tallest mountain and has not erupted in hundreds of years, but scientists think it could erupt at any time. I conclude that Mt. Fuji is a volcanic mountain, so I don't need to change the second statement because it is true."

I Do, and You Help

After modeling how to determine the truth of the first two statements, she invites students to help her with the next two.

"Let's read the next paragraph together," she says. "After we read it, we'll figure out what it tells us about any of the remaining statements."

Miss G. and her students read the paragraph and decide to make the third sentence true by changing *lowest* to *highest*. (See figure 1.3.)

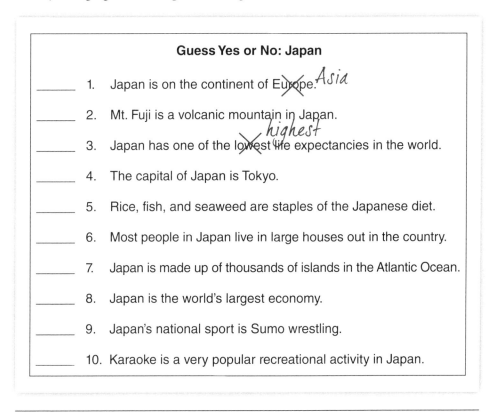

Guess Yes or No: Japan

_____ 1. Japan is on the continent of Europe. *Asia*

_____ 2. Mt. Fuji is a volcanic mountain in Japan.

_____ 3. Japan has one of the ~~lowest~~ *highest* life expectancies in the world.

_____ 4. The capital of Japan is Tokyo.

_____ 5. Rice, fish, and seaweed are staples of the Japanese diet.

_____ 6. Most people in Japan live in large houses out in the country.

_____ 7. Japan is made up of thousands of islands in the Atlantic Ocean.

_____ 8. Japan is the world's largest economy.

_____ 9. Japan's national sport is Sumo wrestling.

_____ 10. Karaoke is a very popular recreational activity in Japan.

Figure 1.3: Sample Guess Yes or No sheet with revisions.

They look at the country map of Japan and conclude that the star next to Tokyo indicates that Tokyo is the capital, which means sentence four is true and doesn't need to be changed.

You Do It Together, and I Help

"Now that you understand what to do, work together to complete the remaining statements. Read the paragraphs together, talk about any visuals, and decide together which statements are true and how to turn the false statements into true statements," Miss G. says to her students.

She circulates among the groups, making sure that students explain their thinking to justify whether a sentence is true or false. She notices one group of students changing a false sentence by simply inserting the word *not*: "Japan is *not* the world's largest economy."

She helps them change the sentence without using the word *not*: "Japan is the world's *third largest* economy."

TIP

Don't let students take the easy way out and use the word not *to make false statements true. Disallowing the word* not *requires students to think about how to make a false statement true.*

She then makes a new rule and announces it to the class: "When making a false sentence true, the word *not* is NOT allowed!"

The Class Debriefs

After the trios finish reading, verifying, and changing sentences, the class regroups and focuses on the last six statements. If students believe that statements were already true, Miss G. has them locate and read aloud the place in the text that confirms these statements. They also read aloud portions of the text that let them decide that statements were false and share their thinking to determine that.

One student says, "You can see on the map that Japan is made up of lots of islands in the Pacific Ocean—not the Atlantic Ocean!"

Students express amazement that seaweed is indeed eaten almost every day in Japan and point out that the article didn't talk about life expectancies in the United States, which they intend to find out. (See figure 1.4 for a sample student-completed sheet.)

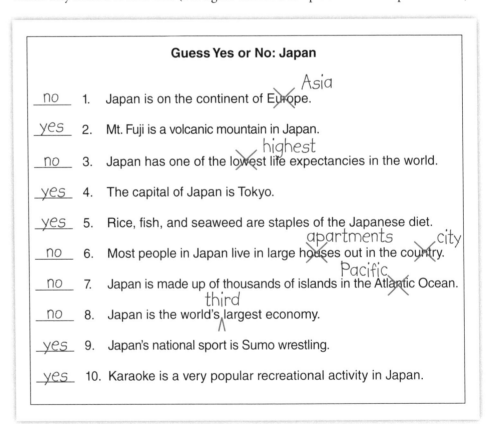

Figure 1.4: Sample student-completed Guess Yes or No sheet.

To conclude the lesson, Miss G. asks students to look back at the article and write one more true statement or find one that they can easily turn into a false statement. She asks students to do this individually and not to tell anyone whether their statement is true or false. When students have had two minutes to write this new statement, she lets several students read theirs to the class and call on other students to guess whether it is true or false and to turn false statements into true statements.

Planning and Teaching a Guess Yes or No Lesson

Create ten statements about the text using key vocabulary, including false statements that can easily be turned into true statements. Write some statements that require students to make logical inferences. Use the following seven steps when teaching a Guess Yes or No lesson. The first time or two, it helps to have ten statements so there are several to use for the "I do, and you watch" and "I do, and you help" modeling. Later, when students do all of them in trios or individually, you may want to have fewer statements.

1. Tell students the purpose of the lesson: "Today we are going to use our close-reading skills to determine which statements are true and which are false, and we are going to use the details from the text to turn false statements into true statements."

2. Have students read each statement with you, and ask students questions to build meaning for vocabulary. Point out morphemic connections students should understand. Help students use the context of the sentence to determine the appropriate meaning of multimeaning words, and help them clarify the meanings of homophones.

3. Have students use pencils to write a *yes* or *no* next to each statement to indicate their guesses. Assure them that they can erase any incorrect guesses and change them to correct guesses as they read.

4. Model ("I do, and you watch"), and then have students work with you ("I do, and you help") to complete the first several statements. Be sure to locate evidence in the text to verify your answers.

5. Have students work in trios to read and decide whether each remaining statement is true or not. Have them turn the false statements into true statements without using the word *not*. Observe their interactions, and intervene and coach as necessary as the students work together ("You do it together, and I help"). Use your observations to formatively assess their close-reading and inferencing skills.

6. Gather your students and have them read each statement and share how their trios turned false statements into true statements. Have them read parts of the text that prove statements are false.

7. Have each student write one or two new sentences that are true or false. Let a few students share their sentences and call on other students to tell if they are true or false and to turn false statements into true statements.

TIP

Creating these statements helps students read carefully and supports the development of close reading.

Guess Yes or No Lessons Across the Year

In subsequent lessons as students demonstrate their ability to make predictions, to support and change their predictions based on information from the text, and to apply this strategy by creating one new true or false statement, you should fade teacher modeling and turn over the responsibility for all ten statements to the trios. Continue, however, to begin every lesson by having students read each statement chorally with you to build academic and subject-area vocabulary. When your observations of the group interaction indicate that most of your students can successfully complete most of the statements most of the time, have students do the lesson independently ("You do, and I watch"). Use the results of this assessment to determine which students can meet the standards and which students need continued work on that skill.

How Guess Yes or No Lessons Teach the Standards

Guess Yes or No lessons teach Reading anchor standard one (CCRA.R.1) because students learn to read closely to determine whether statements are true or false, to make logical inferences, and to cite textual evidence to support their responses. These lessons also teach Reading informational text and Language anchor standards four (RI.4, CCRA.L.4). Before students read, they read the statements together, and the teacher helps them use context and morphemic clues when appropriate to determine word meanings. The lessons teach Speaking and Listening anchor standard one (CCRA. SL.1), as well, because they use a combination of small-group (trios) and teacher-led collaborative conversations with diverse partners to discuss various aspects of the content of the text.

CCSS in a Find It or Figure It Out Lesson

Find It or Figure It Out is a lesson framework you can use with both informational and narrative text. When you lead students through this lesson several times and gradually release responsibility to them, you are helping them learn the reading and speaking and listening skills in the following standards.

Reading

CCRA.R.1: Read closely to determine what the text says explicitly and to make logical inferences from it; cite specific textual evidence when writing or speaking to support conclusions drawn from the text.

Speaking and Listening

CCRA.SL.1: Prepare for and participate effectively in a range of conversations and collaborations with diverse partners, building on others' ideas and expressing their own clearly and persuasively.

Language

CCRA.L.6: Acquire and use accurately a range of general academic and domain-specific words and phrases sufficient for reading, writing, speaking, and listening at the college and career readiness level; demonstrate independence in gathering vocabulary knowledge when encountering an unknown term important to comprehension or expression.

Source: Adapted from NGA & CCSSO, 2010, pp. 10, 22, 25.

CHAPTER 2

Find It or Figure It Out

Have you ever asked your students a question about something they read and had them respond, "I don't know; it didn't say"? Many students are literal when they read. They expect to find all the answers to questions directly in the text. In reality, most of the thinking you do as you read is not literal. Your brain puts information you read together with information you know and figures out many things that the text does not directly state. If you read the weather forecast, and the chances of rain are 100 percent, you figure out that you probably need to rethink your plans for a barbecue this weekend. Figuring out something based on information from the text is *inferring*. Find It or Figure It Out is a lesson framework you can employ to teach your students how to use the information in the text and their prior knowledge to figure things out. The major emphasis in Find It or Figure It Out lessons is teaching students how to make logical inferences and cite textual evidence to support them. Using the gradual release of responsibility model of instruction, Find It or Figure It Out combines student trios and teacher-led collaborative conversations to discuss various aspects of the text's content.

A Sample Find It or Figure It Out Lesson

Mr. E. decides to use Find It or Figure It Out to teach his students how to make and support inferences as they read a section about tropical rain forests in their science texts. He reads the text and constructs prompts for each two-page spread in the book. He makes sure that the answers to the Find It questions are quite literal and that students can find them in the text in a sentence or two. His Figure It Out questions require students to make logical inferences. There are clues that help them figure out the answers.

This is the first Find It or Figure It Out lesson this class has experienced. Mr. E. follows the gradual release of responsibility model of instruction when teaching comprehension lessons. Working with the whole class, he establishes the purpose for the lesson, builds meaning for important vocabulary, and models how to answer one question. He then asks the whole class to help him answer the second question. Next, the class works in trios to answer the remaining questions. He has organized the trios so each has a range of reading levels and has also tried to put students together who like to work with one another.

Purpose Setting and Vocabulary Building

TIP

Small groups in elementary classrooms work best if the group size is not too large. When working together in trios, all three students participate, and rarely does anyone sit on the sidelines.

The lesson begins with the students gathering in their assigned trios. Mr. E. hands one copy of the Find It or Figure It Out: Tropical Rain Forests question sheet (see figure 2.1) to each trio, and the person who gets the sheet quickly positions him- or herself between the other two. He gives the other two students small sticky notes in two different colors. Next, he establishes the lesson purpose.

Find It or Figure It Out: Tropical Rain Forests

1. Figure out if there are any rain forests in Africa and Australia. (pp. 4–5)

2. Find out the average high and low temperatures in a tropical rain forest and the average amount of rain. (pp. 6–7)

3. Figure out how a forest is like a cake. (pp. 8–9)

4. Figure out which layer of the forest is as tall as many adults. (pp. 10–11)

5. Figure out which part of a rain forest is hard to walk through. (pp. 12–13)

6. Find out what epiphytes are and how they help trees. (pp. 14–15)

Figure 2.1: Sample Find It or Figure It Out: Tropical Rain Forests question sheet.

He says, "Shortly, I am going to give you a piece to read about tropical rain forests. As you read it, you are going to find the answers to some questions and figure out the answers to others. The answers to the Find It questions will be right there on the page. When you find these answers, you will put a green sticky note on them to show where you found them. The answers to the Figure It Out questions will not be right there on the page, but there will be clues in the text to help you figure them out. You are going to use the yellow sticky notes to mark the details from the text that are clues you used to answer the Figure It Out questions. Before we start reading about tropical rain forests, however, we need to use our collective class knowledge to build meanings for some key words. Read the first question with me, and tell me what you think the key vocabulary words are."

The class reads the first sentence chorally: "Figure out if there are any rain forests in Africa and Australia." The students decide that *rain forests*, *Africa*, and *Australia* are important vocabulary words. Mr. E. directs their attention to the world map, and the students identify Africa and Australia. He then tells them that a rain forest is a forest that gets a lot of rain. When Mr. E. asks if anyone has ever seen a rain forest, one student describes the movie *FernGully: The Last Rainforest*. Other students report having seen programs on the Discovery Channel about rain forests. Some suggest finding cool videos on YouTube, and Mr. E. says that is a good idea and he will investigate.

Next, the class reads the second sentence chorally: "Find out the average high and low temperatures in a tropical rain forest and the average amount of rain." The students decide that *high and low temperatures* and *tropical* are important vocabulary words. Mr. E. leads them to talk about the high and low temperatures where they live and then writes the words *tropics* and *tropical* on the board. He asks students to tell how these words are related. Students volunteer that they think the *tropics* are a place where it gets very hot and that *tropical* describes a rain forest in the tropics that is probably very hot.

Together, the students read the remaining sentences. They jointly decide on key vocabulary words and share their collective knowledge. No one knows what *epiphytes* are, and Mr. E. says their reading will help them figure that out. He has the students pronounce the word *epiphytes* several times and points out that *ph* has the sound they know from words such as *phone* and *elephant*.

I Do, and You Watch

Once the students have read all the sentences chorally, and Mr. E. has developed meanings and pronunciations for vocabulary, he hands the text to the middle person in each trio.

He says, "Now, I am going to show you how I figure out the answer to the first question: 'Figure out if there are any rain forests in Africa and Australia.' I am going to read the page aloud and tell you what the clues are that helped me figure it out."

Mr. E. reads the page aloud and then thinks aloud, saying, "'The most important rain forests are near the equator, in the area between the Tropic of Cancer and the Tropic of Capricorn.' It doesn't say anywhere if there are tropical rain forests in Africa and Australia. But I can use the information in the sentences and the map to figure it out. When I look at the map on this page, I see that Africa and Australia are between the Tropic of Cancer and the Tropic of Capricorn. When I put that map information together with what I read in this sentence, I can figure out that there are tropical rain forests in both Africa and Australia. Let's put a yellow sticky note on this sentence and another on the map to mark the clues I used to figure out the answer."

When the trios have marked the clues with yellow sticky notes, Mr. E. draws their attention to the second question.

I Do, and You Help

He and the class read it together: "Find out the average high and low temperatures in a tropical rain forest and the average amount of rain."

He says, "Question two is a Find It question. We need to find two facts: the average high and low temperatures and the average rainfall in a tropical rain forest. Read these two pages with me, and help me find these facts."

The students and Mr. E. read the two pages chorally: "The temperature rarely goes above 93 degrees or drops below 68 degrees. At least eighty inches of rain falls each year." Students eagerly volunteer the answers to both questions. They mark these two sentences with green sticky notes.

TIP

Seizing every opportunity to point out morphological relationships between words will help your students rapidly increase the size of their meaning vocabularies.

TIP

When reading on their own, students often skip over words they can't immediately pronounce. Use the vocabulary introduction time to help them with both meanings and pronunciations.

TIP

Students work together and interact more when they have just one copy of the text.

TIP

The "You do it together, and I help" phase of the lesson is a perfect time to listen in on the discussions your students are having and formatively assess how they are thinking and what misunderstandings they may have.

You Do It Together, and I Help

Before letting the trios read and work together to answer the remaining questions, Mr. E. makes sure that they identify questions three, four, and five as Figure It Out questions and question six as a Find It question.

He says, "Begin by writing the answers to the first two questions that we did together on your Find It or Figure It Out question sheet. Then, read each question and find or figure out the answer. For the Figure It Out questions, explain to each other which sentences and pictures have clues and how these clues help you figure it out. Mark them with yellow sticky notes, and write the answer on your sheet. For question six, you will need to find the sentences that tell you what epiphytes are and how epiphytes help trees. Use your green sticky notes to mark the places where you found these answers."

As the students work together, Mr. E. circulates the room and reminds students to explain to each other where they found answers and which sentences in the text provided clues that helped them figure out answers not right there on the page.

The Class Debriefs

The class gathers together, and students share their answers to the questions and where they placed their sticky notes. For the Figure It Out questions, Mr. E. leads students to share their thinking and explain how they used the text clues to figure out the answers.

Mr. E. asks students to look back through the pages read and create one more Find It question and one more Figure It Out question. They write their two questions and mark the places where they found answers or clues with yellow and green sticky notes. Mr. E. concludes the lesson by letting a few students volunteer their questions and the thinking and details they used to answer the questions.

Planning and Teaching a Find It or Figure It Out Lesson

Read the informational or narrative text and come up with Find It or Figure It Out questions. Find It questions should be literal. Students should find the answer to the question in a sentence or two. Figure It Out questions should have clues to help students figure out the answer. Include one or two questions for each page or two-page spread. Use the following seven steps when teaching a Find It or Figure It Out lesson.

1. Tell students the purpose of the lesson: "When you read, you get information in two ways. Some information is easy to find because it is right there on the page. Other information is not right there on the page, but if you look for clues, you can figure out the answer. Today, we are going to use our Find It or Figure It Out strategies to answer some questions about _____."

2. Have students read each question chorally with you and build meanings for key vocabulary. Having students tell you what they think the important vocabulary is will help them learn how to identify key vocabulary. Seize every opportunity to point out morphological relations among words. Make sure students can pronounce all words, and remind them of similar words that will help them pronounce difficult words.

3. Model for students what you want them to do by using the "I do, and you watch" phase for the first question. Read the pages aloud, answer the

question, and show where you found the answer or clues to help you figure it out. Explain how you used your brain and the clues to figure out answers.

4. For the second question, use the "I do, and you help" phase. Have students read the text with you and locate where they found answers or clues and explain their thinking.

5. Have students work in trios to complete the remaining questions. Circulate among your students, and be sure they locate the evidence in the text that helps them determine the answers and explain their thinking. Have them use small sticky notes to mark the places where they found the answers and the clues they used to figure out answers. Eavesdrop on the trios' interactions to make formative assessments of students' ability to make inferences.

6. Gather your students and have them answer the questions and explain where they found answers and clues and how their brains used the clues to figure out the answers.

7. Have students write a new Find It question and a new Figure It Out question. Share some of these with the whole class as time permits.

Find It or Figure It Out Lessons Across the Year

In subsequent lessons, as students demonstrate their ability to answer literal and inferential questions and to support their answers with evidence from the text, you should fade your modeling and turn over the responsibility for all questions to the trios. Continue, however, to begin every lesson by having students read each statement chorally with you and providing instruction on word meanings and pronunciations. When your observations of each trio's interactions indicate that most of your students have learned to make logical inferences and to support those inferences with evidence from the text, have students answer the questions independently ("You do, and I watch"). Use the assessment results to determine which students meet the standards and which need more work on that skill.

To help students apply their inferencing skills when reading on their own, remind students as they are about to begin their independent reading time to use clues to figure out things the author does not directly state. When independent reading time is over, take a few minutes to let students volunteer one clue they figured out, read the parts of the text that led them to the inference, and explain their thinking.

How Find It or Figure It Out Lessons Teach the Standards

Find It or Figure It Out lessons teach Reading anchor standard one (CCRA.R.1) because students learn how to make logical inferences and to cite textual evidence to support the inferences they make. The lesson framework teaches Speaking and Listening anchor standard one (CCRA.SL.1) as well, because students participate in collaborative conversations with diverse partners both in their small groups and with the whole class. These lessons also teach Language anchor standard six (CCRA.L.6), because the statements include general academic and domain-specific words and phrases from the text, and the teacher builds meanings as students read these together before reading the text.

CCSS in a Question It Lesson

Question It is a lesson framework to use with a short, dense, and challenging text. When you lead students through this lesson several times and gradually release responsibility to them, you are helping them learn the reading, speaking and listening, and language skills in the following standards.

Reading

CCRA.R.1: Read closely to determine what the text says explicitly and to make logical inferences from it; cite specific textual evidence when writing or speaking to support conclusions drawn from the text.

Speaking and Listening

CCRA.SL.1: Prepare for and participate effectively in a range of conversations and collaborations with diverse partners, building on others' ideas and expressing their own clearly and persuasively.

Language

CCRA.L.6: Acquire and use accurately a range of general academic and domain-specific words and phrases sufficient for reading, writing, speaking, and listening at the college and career readiness level; demonstrate independence in gathering vocabulary knowledge when encountering an unknown term important to comprehension or expression.

Source: Adapted from NGA & CCSSO, 2010, pp. 10, 22, 25.

CHAPTER 3

Question It

When most of us think of reading, we think of spending leisure time with a book, magazine, newspaper, or website for pleasure or self-improvement. There is, however, a specific type of reading that demands a different approach: short, dense, and challenging texts. Think of being faced with directions for electronics with "some assembly required," a new and complicated recipe for a dish, a contract we fear to sign but must, or instructions for filling out taxes. We recognize the need to read these texts differently. We slow down, reading deliberately line by line, sentence by sentence, or sometimes even word by word. If we are not sure we understand a sentence, we reread it, possibly several times. We are alert for implications and do our best to read between the lines to draw any logical inferences we are justified in making. This close reading that brief but difficult texts require also has periodic applications in our more casual reading. When perusing a literary or informational text, we occasionally encounter a section we are interested in whose meaning initially eludes us. So we shift to a lower gear and read closely for a bit before returning to a more normal pace and state of attentiveness. In our experience, schools have worked hard to teach students how to do typical reading but have spent relatively little time or effort teaching them how to read closely. Question It is a comprehension lesson framework that teaches students how to do this close reading.

The major emphasis in Question It is teaching students to read closely until they have exhausted what a short, dense, and challenging text says explicitly or implicitly about a subject. Beginning in third grade, with Reading literature and informational text standards one (RL.3.1 and RI.3.1), students must be able to cite textual evidence to support the questions they pose when required to do so: "Ask and answer questions to demonstrate understanding of a text, referring explicitly to the text as the basis for the answers" (NGA & CCSSO, 2010, pp. 11, 14). In Question It, the teacher pre-teaches a few general academic and domain-specific words and phrases from the text to ensure students can read it closely with comprehension. Using the gradual release of responsibility model of instruction, Question It combines student trios and teacher-led collaborative conversations to discuss various aspects of the text's content.

TIP

In most schools, Question It is a lesson framework students can be successful with beginning in the spring of second grade and moving on up through the grades.

A Sample Question It Lesson

This is the fourth Question It lesson Mrs. R.'s class has experienced. Because a handful of students still struggled with the lesson the last time she taught it, Mrs. R. continues with the full set of procedures from the gradual release of responsibility model of instruction in this lesson as she did in the first three lessons.

Purpose Setting and Vocabulary Building

Mrs. R. says, "In a few minutes, I'm going to have you open your social studies books and read a short excerpt. Before you start reading, I will give you a word or phrase from the text. Your job will be to come up with as many questions as possible that the word or phrase is the answer to."

Several students raise their hands and say they remember this lesson from when Mrs. R. has taught it before. One student even recollects that the lesson is called Question It.

Mrs. R. continues, "Before I have you read, I want to make sure you understand some vocabulary terms in the passage. What is the U.S. Constitution?"

Students recall from previous lessons in the current social studies unit that the U.S. Constitution is a written document that spells out the U.S. government's laws. Mrs. R. asks if anyone knows how old the Constitution is. No one remembers the exact year it was ratified, but several students agree it was over two hundred years ago. Mrs. R. tells them they are correct and that the year of ratification was 1789. She then asks, "What is an amendment to the Constitution?"

When no one answers, she explains that an amendment is something written and added to the Constitution in order to change it. She says, "The section you are going to read today is about amendments to the U.S. Constitution."

I Do, and You Watch

Mrs. R. writes the word *citizen* on the chalkboard. (Mrs. R. could also use a whiteboard, a projector, or any other means to display the word big enough for students to see.)

She asks the students to open their social studies books to the two pages that explain how the U.S. Constitution can be and has been changed. She tells them she is going to read the section to herself until it tells her something about a citizen. When she gets there, she is going to ask a question that the book answers about the word *citizen*. She reads silently until she comes to a place in the second paragraph.

She tells them exactly where she is in the text and then poses a question: "When someone is born in the United States, what does that make him or her?"

"A citizen," many students respond.

"All right," she says, "I've asked one question that *citizen* is the answer to."

I Do, and You Help

She asks, "Can any of you ask another question about this section that *citizen* is the answer to?"

After two students try to ask a good question and are unable to do so, one student asks, "What is a person who has followed the law to become a naturalized citizen?"

TIP

Repetition of the lesson framework over time along with the gradual release of responsibility model will help reduce the number of students who might still have difficulty with the task when it comes time to work the task alone. Then, the teacher can identify any struggling students and pull them aside in a group to provide extra help.

Mrs. R. says, "Yes, the answer to that question is a *citizen*." Mrs. R. turns to the class as a whole and asks, "Where does the text tell us that the answer to this question is a *citizen*?"

A girl volunteers to try. She reads aloud the explanation of *naturalization* and explains that if completed properly the person becomes an American citizen.

"Good job," says Mrs. R., and several students nod.

"Now," she says to the class, "you and I have asked two questions with *citizen* as the answer."

During the last Question It lesson, Mrs. R. noticed that some students in several trios were having difficulty formulating questions. This observation led her to continue using the "I do, and you watch" and "I do, and you help" phases in this lesson to model how to come up with the questions. Then, she has the students get together in their trios.

You Do It Together, and I Help

Mrs. R. has the students get into their trios. Earlier in the year, she assigned her students to trios with a range of reading levels, and the members work well with one another. After the first time she used the trios, she switched two students between trios to improve their work ethic. Because her students are now accustomed to working together in trios, she does not feel the need for each trio to have just one copy of the text. She allows each student to keep his or her social studies book open to the section on changing the U.S. Constitution.

Mrs. R. estimates how many minutes to give the trios to complete the task and communicates it to them.

She displays the word *amendment* and tells her students, "Quickly pick a scribe for your trio. Then, for ten minutes, have the scribe write as many questions as your trio can think of that this section of the book answers with the word *amendment*. Questions with the answer in plural form—*amendments*—will also count. I am going to walk around and help you when you need me to. I wonder which trio will ask the most questions. Your ten minutes start now."

The Class Debriefs

When the time limit is up, Mrs. R. has each trio read one of its questions, and she keeps a tally of how many different questions the students share. The first trio contributes the question, "Why doesn't the person who loses the presidential election become the vice president?"

Mrs. R. turns to the class and asks, "What is the answer the book gives us to this question?"

A student in a different trio responds, "An amendment."

"Yes," agrees Mrs. R., "an amendment changed that from the original Constitution. Very good, that's one question. It is the next trio's turn to read one of its questions."

One student reads, "What made slavery illegal in the United States?"

"What is the book's answer to this question?" Mrs. R. asks the other students.

"An amendment," one volunteers.

"Correct," she says. "Those are two questions."

TIP

The perfect time to use formative assessment and listen in on trios' thinking is when they are working together.

TIP

The time limit you provide depends on the text's length and difficulty and how many previous Question It lessons you've taught. Estimate what the best time limit will be under your specific circumstances.

The trios continue to alternate sharing until they've shared all questions. The class helps Mrs. R. decide whether each question should count. For example, one trio shares a question that is similar to a question that another trio shared. Everyone agrees only the first question should count. The last unique question a trio has after every other trio has passed is "What is the Bill of Rights?"

"What is the answer, class?" asks Mrs. R.

"Amendments," say several students at once.

"That's right!" she exclaims. She congratulates them for asking all twelve questions she had thought of, so she has none to add to the total. The class gives themselves a silent cheer for coming up with twelve different questions for the passage that could be answered with the word *amendment* or *amendments*.

Mrs. R. ends the day's lesson by discussing with the class how the U.S. Constitution is amended and which amendments they think were probably the most important ones. She is pleased that their comments and questions reveal that they have read the text closely. Because everyone did reasonably well in this lesson, Mrs. R. decides that the next time she uses Question It, she can begin it with the "You do it together, and I help" phase.

Planning and Teaching a Question It Lesson

Select a short, dense text that will be challenging for many of your students and that you would like everyone to read closely. The text you choose may stand alone or be an excerpt from a longer text, and it should have at least one explicit name, word, or phrase for you to display as the answer to an adequate number of questions for an effective Question It lesson. Decide on two or three vocabulary terms that are the most important for students to know when reading the text to introduce beforehand. Early Question It lessons will work better if the text you select is like the one the teacher chose in the sample lesson. In that lesson, everything the text said about amendments was explicit. Once your students are comfortable with the Question It lesson framework, they can work successfully with a text that has both explicit and implicit references to whatever name, word, or phrase you have chosen to focus the lesson on. Use the following six steps when teaching a Question It lesson.

1. Tell students the purpose of the lesson: they are going to read carefully and ask as many different questions as they can think of that the text answers with the name, word, or phrase you have displayed.

2. Teach or review the meanings of two or three vocabulary terms you believe may prevent some of your students from comprehending the text well.

3. For the first several Question It lessons, use the "I do, and you watch" and "I do, and you help" phases to model what you want students to do and to get them off to a successful start. In these phases, you can employ the same text they will read during "You do it together, and I help," but use a different name, word, or phrase from the one you will display for the students to seek questions for.

4. Have students work together in trios to come up with questions that the word you are focusing on answers ("You do it together, and I help"). Assign (or let students choose) a scribe for each trio so only one student writes down responses for the group.

5. Circulate among the trios and conduct formative assessments by listening in on their interactions. Encourage students to ask each other for evidence from the text and an explanation whenever the text doesn't explicitly answer the question. This will prepare the trio to defend its questions as good ones when the whole class gathers to tally the questions.

6. Assemble the class, and have trios take turns sharing questions. When a trio suggests a question that isn't explicit in the text, ask for a volunteer to read the part of the text that question is based on and explain the trio's thinking behind the question. If you and the class do not agree that there is evidence the question can be answered based on the text, do not count it in your running tally. Once the trios have exhausted the questions they wrote, ask any others that you have thought of, and make it clear why they are countable questions.

Question It Lessons Across the Year

In later Question It lessons, as students demonstrate their ability to ask questions that the text would answer with the displayed term, gradually fade to independence where "You do, and I watch" is the only procedure you use. Eventually, you'll want to be able to present a grade-appropriate text to your class that is short, dense, and challenging and have each student read it closely and then respond well orally or in writing to the general question, "What does this text tell us about _____?"

How Question It Lessons Teach the Standards

Question It lessons teach Reading anchor standard one (CCRA.R.1) because the major emphasis in Question It is teaching students to read closely until they have exhausted what a short, dense, and challenging text says explicitly or implicitly about a subject. Additionally, beginning in third grade, they are expected to cite explicit textual evidence to support that their questions have that answer. These lessons also teach Language anchor standard six (CCRA.L.6), because Question It has the teacher preteach a few general academic and domain-specific words and phrases from the text that are essential for students to read it closely with comprehension. The lessons teach Speaking and Listening anchor standard one (CCRA.SL.1) because the students collaborate with the teacher in the second phase and work together in the third phase of the gradual release of responsibility model.

CCSS in a Gist Lesson

Gist is a lesson framework for use with a short text. When you lead students through this lesson several times and gradually release responsibility to them, you are helping them learn the reading and speaking and listening skills in the following standards.

Reading
CCRA.R.1: Read closely to determine what the text says explicitly and to make logical inferences from it; cite specific textual evidence when writing or speaking to support conclusions drawn from the text.
CCRA.R.2: Determine central ideas or themes of a text, and analyze their development; summarize the key supporting details and ideas.

Speaking and Listening
CCRA.SL.1: Prepare for and participate effectively in a range of conversations and collaborations with diverse partners, building on others' ideas and expressing their own clearly and persuasively.

Source: Adapted from NGA & CCSSO, 2010, pp. 10, 22.

CHAPTER 4

Gist

When friends start to tell you about a movie they've seen or a book they've read, and it seems like they are going to talk for a while, you may ask them just to give you the gist. The *gist* is the main part or essence of something. It is the nub, the core. In reading, a *gist* is a one-sentence summary of the text (Cunningham & Moore, 1986). In order for readers to compose a good gist, they must be sensitive to the various clues in the text that indicate which ideas are most central and important. For example, an idea referred to throughout a text is more central and important than an idea only communicated in one place. Being able to grasp the gist of a text is essential. To comprehend a text, readers need to understand more than each sentence or paragraph. The reader must also understand what those sentences and paragraphs add up to.

The major emphasis in Gist lessons is helping students identify central and key ideas in a particular text. Gist lessons also teach students to read closely until they have exhausted what a short text says explicitly or implicitly about a subject. Beginning in third grade, with Reading for literature and informational text standards one (RL.3.1 and RI.3.1), students must be able to cite textual evidence to explain any words in their Gist statements that you or another student questions: "Ask and answer questions to demonstrate understanding of a text, referring explicitly to the text as the basis for the answers" (NGA & CCSSO, 2010, pp. 11, 14). Using the gradual release of responsibility model of instruction, Gist lessons combine student trios and teacher-led collaborative conversations to discuss various aspects of the text's content.

A Sample Gist Lesson

This is the first Gist lesson this class has experienced. Because Gist is challenging for most students, Mr. O. will follow the gradual release of responsibility model of instruction through a series of Gist lessons. For the first few Gist lessons, he will only use the "I do, and you watch" and "I do, and you help" steps.

Purpose Setting

Mr. O. says, "Today, we're going to work on how to summarize a passage in one sentence. This will be hard work because the passage has 176 words in it, but the one-sentence summary we write can't have more than fourteen words in it. In a minute, I am going to show you the beginning of the text. We'll start by summarizing just this first part. Then, I'll show you both the first and second parts, and we'll summarize those in one sentence. Finally, I'll let you see the entire passage, and we'll try to summarize it all in a sentence with fourteen or fewer words."

I Do, and You Watch

Mr. O. displays the first part of the short text he has chosen to use in this lesson and asks the students to read it to themselves. (For example, see *The 100 Greatest Track and Field Battles of the Twentieth Century*; Hollobaugh, 2012.)

"Bob Beamon was an American track-and-field athlete. His event was the men's long jump. He was one of two athletes who represented the United States in the 1968 Olympics in Mexico City. He was the overall favorite to win the gold medal."

When they have finished reading it, he says, "I am going to write a Gist statement for this part of the text, so you can see how it works."

Mr. O. hides the text and displays fourteen blanks on a projector. (Mr. O. could also use a whiteboard, a chalkboard, or any other means to display the blanks big enough for students to see.) He thinks out loud: "It seems pretty important to give his name."

He writes *Bob Beamon* in the first two blanks.

He continues, "I think I should also include that he was in the 1968 Olympics in Mexico City."

He writes those words in the next eight blanks and counts how many blanks he has left—four. (See figure 4.1.)

> **TIP**
>
> *Gist is an instructional strategy for use in grades 2 and up. Students get gradually better at reading and writing longer sentences as they move up through the grades. A good rule of thumb for the length of the summary sentence is the students' grade plus ten. This sample lesson is taking place in a fourth-grade classroom, so the maximum number of words in the Gist statement is fourteen.*

Bob	Beamon	was
in	the	1968
Olympics	in	Mexico
City		

Figure 4.1: Sample Gist statement.

"There are lots of events in the Olympics," he says. "I think it's important to say that he was in the long jump. It sounds better to me to put that in before I tell about the Olympics."

He removes the four blanks at the end, puts a caret (^) between *was* and *in the 1968 Olympics*, inserts four blanks above the caret, and writes *in the long jump* in those blanks. (See figure 4.2.)

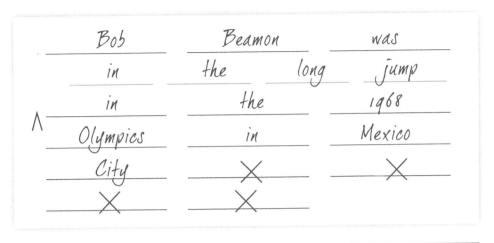

Figure 4.2: Sample Gist statement with revisions.

He says, "Uh oh, I don't have any blanks left, but I haven't told that he represented the United States. I think that's very important, don't you? What can I do about that? You know, I think it's more significant that he was on our Olympic team than where the Olympics took place that year."

He removes the three blanks with the words *in Mexico City* in them. Then, he places a caret between *was* and *in the long jump*, inserts three blanks above the caret, and writes *for the United States* in those blanks. He looks at what he has written. (See figure 4.3.)

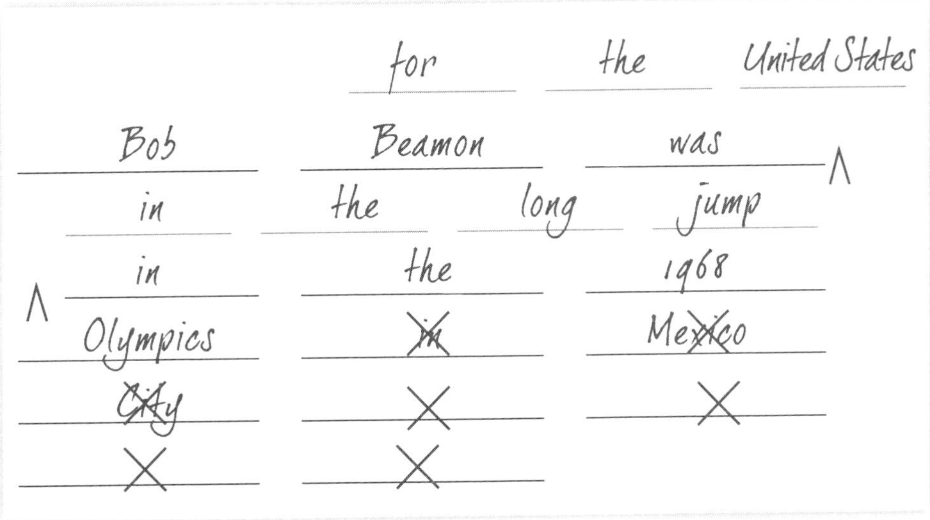

Figure 4.3: Sample Gist statement with revisions.

"I don't like *was* anymore. I'm going to put a word there that tells what he actually did for the United States. He *competed* for the United States in the Olympics," he says.

He removes the word *was* from the blank and writes in *competed* instead. Mr. O. leaves his summary sentence displayed and also displays the first part of the text again, saying, "Look at my Gist statement. Do you see how I summarized the most important ideas in the beginning of the passage?" (See figure 4.4.)

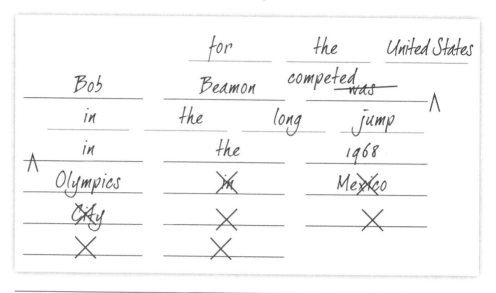

Figure 4.4: Sample completed Gist statement.

Mr. O. asks if anyone has a suggestion to make his Gist statement better. One student asks if the Olympics has a women's long jump event. When Mr. O. says it does, the student says he thinks the summary sentence should say "in the *men's* long jump." He asks if anyone can figure out how to remove a word somewhere so he can add *men's*, but no one can. Finally, a student says that since *Bob* is a man's name, they don't need to add *men's*. Mr. O. and most students nod in agreement.

I Do, and You Help

Mr. O. says, "Now, I am going to write a Gist statement for the first two parts of the text. But this time, I want you to help me decide what to write and when I need to make changes."

Mr. O. displays the first two parts of the text and asks the students to read it to themselves. He reminds them to read it carefully, since he will hide the text while they work on the Gist statement.

"Bob Beamon was an American athlete in track and field. His event was the men's long jump. He was one of two athletes who represented the United States in the 1968 Olympics in Mexico City. He was the overall favorite to win the gold medal. He barely made it to the finals because he scratched twice before making a jump that was good enough. The other finalists were men who had won the two previous Olympic gold medals and a third man who had won the bronze medal twice. In the finals on October 18, Beamon made a great jump to win the gold medal."

Mr. O. hides the text and displays fourteen blanks. He asks, "Who can start our Gist statement?"

TIP

Gist always works better when students work on their Gist statements from memory. Students will read the text more carefully if they know they will be working from memory, and they are more likely to use words like competed *in their Gist statements that aren't in the text. If students begin arguing over what the text says, show them the text so far and let them read it again, but hide it once more while they work on their summary sentence.*

After a pause, a student suggests, "Let's start with his name again."

Mr. O. writes *Bob Beamon* in the first two blanks. He says, "Let's talk about what you think are the most important things to make sure we include in our summary sentence."

After a discussion, the students agree that they still should tell that he was in the 1968 Olympics and his event was the long jump. He adds those words to the statement. (See figure 4.5.)

Bob	Beamon	was
in	the	long
jump	in	the
1968	Olympics	

Figure 4.5: Sample Gist statement.

"We have to tell that he won!" exclaims a student.

So, Mr. O. erases *was in*, writes *won*, and adds a blank at the end. Another student says it wasn't just that he won, but that he won a *gold medal*. Finally, Mr. O. asks if he should include what country Beamon represented. Students agree he should. When they can't figure out how to say that in the two blanks they have left, he suggests adding *American Bob Beamon* at the beginning and rearranging the clauses at the end. The students relax, clearly impressed with the Gist statement they have helped compose. (See figure 4.6.)

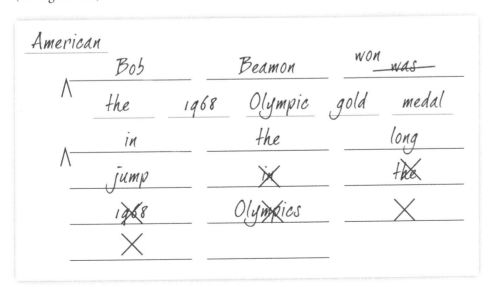

Figure 4.6: Sample Gist statement with revisions.

TIP

The task in a Gist lesson is especially challenging, and the "I do, and you help" phase of the gradual release of responsibility model is particularly valuable. Consequently, this sample lesson has no "You do it together, and I help" section. With Gist, for a number of lessons, many students will likely disengage by the end of "I do, and you help." Their cognitive workload is high! When your students successfully and efficiently help you compose good Gist statements, reveal the whole text from the beginning and complete the "I do, and you help" phase. Eventually, they should compose Gist statements in small groups for a text displayed as a whole. At that point, it will probably be best to have the "You do it together, and I help" phase comprise the entire Gist lesson because of how long it is likely to take and how taxing it is likely to be for many students.

Mr. O. says, "Very good. You did it and with a blank left over! Now, let's write one more Gist statement. This time, we'll summarize the whole text."

"Bob Beamon was an American athlete in track and field. His event was the men's long jump. He was one of two athletes who represented the United States in the 1968 Olympics in Mexico City. He was the overall favorite to win the gold medal. He barely made it to the finals because he scratched twice before making a jump that was good enough. The other finalists were men who had won the two previous Olympic gold medals and a third man who had won the bronze medal twice. In the finals on October 18, Beamon made a great jump to win the gold medal. He made his running approach and then jumped into the sand pit. He seemed to fly. When he landed and fell forward, he was past the camera that had been set up. The judges had to measure his jump with a tape measure. He had jumped 29 feet 2½ inches and broken the world record by almost two feet! Everyone was amazed, including him. His world record stood for twenty-three years."

By this time, many of the students are wearing down. Mr. O. helps them more with this Gist statement than the previous one to speed up the process. Before long, they've completed the lesson. (See figure 4.7.)

American	Bob	Beamon
broke	the	long
jump's	world	record
in	the	1968
Olympics		

Figure 4.7: Sample completed Gist statement.

The Class Debriefs

Mr. O. praises the students highly for their hard work in helping him and asks them what they think about the final Gist statement. Several students express pride in how well they think the Gist statement captures the entire text's meaning in so few words. Mr. O. smiles broadly, and says, "Before long, each of you will be better at reading a text and deciding what will be most important to include in a Gist if you are asked to tell or write one!"

Planning and Teaching a Gist Lesson

Select a short text from which you want your students to identify central and key ideas. The text you choose may stand alone or be an excerpt from a longer text. Divide it into three parts. Use the following four steps when teaching a Gist lesson.

1. Tell students the purpose of the lesson. Explain that you are going to gradually reveal a short text to them, one part at a time, until they can see it all. Each time you show them more of it, they will create a one-sentence summary of the passage so far.

2. For the first few Gist lessons, start with "I do, and you watch" to model your thinking as you write a one-sentence summary for the first part of the text. For the next several Gist lessons, start with "I do, and you help."

3. When using Gist to teach students how to comprehend the main idea of a text, the most important phase of the gradual release of responsibility model is "I do, and you help." "I do, and you help" should be the entire format of Gist lessons until you feel your students no longer benefit from working on the passage in parts. In other words, during the last Gist lessons you teach using the "I do, and you help" phase, you show your students the entire short text at the beginning of the lesson, and they help you compose a Gist statement for the complete passage. You no longer reveal the text in stages.

4. Once your students as a whole group have success with summarizing a short text in one sentence (twelve or more words, depending on their grade), put them in trios to do that same task ("You do it together, and I help"). Display or distribute two or three short texts and have the trios compose a Gist statement of the same length for each one. End that day's lesson by having trios share their Gist statements for each text and discuss differences.

Gist Lessons Across the Year

When you are confident that almost every student will be successful composing a Gist statement, fade instruction to the "You do, and I watch" phase. Eventually, you'll want to be able to give one or more grade-appropriate texts to your class that are short, dense, and challenging and have every student independently write a good one-sentence summary.

How Gist Lessons Teach the Standards

Gist teaches Reading anchor standard two (CCRA.R.2), because its major emphasis is helping students learn to be sensitive to which ideas seem most central and key in a particular text. It also teaches Reading anchor standard one (CCRA.R.1), because it focuses on teaching students to read closely until they have exhausted everything important a short text says explicitly or implicitly about a subject. Beginning in third grade, students must also be able to cite textual evidence and explain any words in their Gist statements that you or another student questions. Because it is taught with the gradual release of responsibility model, Gist also teaches Speaking and Listening anchor standard one (CCRA.SL.1). Students engage in whole-group and small-group conversations with their teacher and peers to discuss what ideas are most central and important in a text.

CCSS in a Themes, Morals, and Lessons Learned Lesson

Themes, Morals, and Lessons Learned is a lesson framework to teach students to identify major characters, settings, and events in a narrative; to think about characters' actions; and to infer a theme, moral, or lesson. When you lead students through this lesson several times and gradually release responsibility to them, you are helping them learn the reading and speaking and listening skills in the following standards.

Reading

CCRA.R.1: Read closely to determine what the text says explicitly and to make logical inferences from it; cite specific textual evidence when writing or speaking to support conclusions drawn from the text.

CCRA.R.2: Determine central ideas or themes of a text, and analyze their development; summarize the key supporting details and ideas.

CCRA.R.3: Analyze how and why individuals, events, or ideas develop and interact over the course of a text.

Speaking and Listening

CCRA.SL.1: Prepare for and participate effectively in a range of conversations and collaborations with diverse partners, building on others' ideas and expressing their own clearly and persuasively.

Source: Adapted from NGA & CCSSO, 2010, pp. 10, 22.

CHAPTER 5

Themes, Morals, and Lessons Learned

When we read an informational text on a topic we are interested in, we can usually recall the main ideas we learned about that topic years later. When reading narratives—stories, plays, and poems—what we tend to remember are the characters and major events in the plot. Often, we also remember some big ideas we constructed about life. After reading Charles Dickens's *A Tale of Two Cities*, you might conclude that the huge wealth differences between the few rich aristocrats and the many poor workers were not only unfair but immoral. Robert Frost's "The Road Not Taken" may lead you to conclude that conformity is not always the best route. Our takeaway after reading a narrative is often a lesson we apply to our own lives. Reading literature standard two (RL.2) focuses on these themes, morals, or lessons learned from narrative text (see NGA & CCSSO, 2010, p. 11). Third graders are expected to "recount stories, including fables, folktales, and myths from diverse cultures; determine the central message, lesson, or moral and explain how it is conveyed through key details in the text" (RL.3.2; NGA & CCSSO, 2010, p. 12). Fifth graders are expected to "determine a theme of a story, drama, or poem from details in the text, including how characters in a story or drama respond to challenges or how the speaker in a poem reflects upon a topic; summarize the text" (RL.5.2; NGA & CCSSO, 2010, p. 12). These are lofty goals for students who are eight to ten years old! Yet, it is this very kind of critical thinking that adults do when they read.

Before you can think about what you can learn from a story, you have to have a clear understanding of what happened. Reading anchor standard standard three (CCRA.R.3) states that readers should be able to "analyze how and why individuals, events, or ideas develop and interact over the course of a text" (NGA & CCSSO, 2010, p. 10). As we read narratives, we ask ourselves, "Who did what to whom? And when and where did these events occur?" In other words, we keep up with characters, settings, and plot.

Themes, Morals, and Lessons Learned explores how to scaffold students' ability to focus on characters, settings, events, and plot and think about themes, morals, and lessons from the stories, plays, and poems. In part one of the lesson, students create a story map, which focuses their attention on characters, settings, and events. In part two, students reread the text to decide what the takeaway is—what can you learn from this story that you can apply to your own life?

In Themes, Morals, and Lessons Learned, students learn to make logical inferences about characters' actions and traits and cite textual evidence to support the inferences they make. Creating a story map focuses student attention on important characters, settings, and events in narratives.

All stories, biographies, and plays have characters, settings, and events. Some of these narratives also have a clear theme, moral, or lesson. You can use any narrative for the story map part of the lesson. To teach your students how to infer themes, morals, and lessons learned, however, you need a narrative that clearly illustrates those points. To plan your lessons, look at the stories, poems, and plays you plan to have your students read, and think about some of the character traits we try to develop in our students. Eve Bunting's *A Day's Work* and Diane deGroat's *Liar, Liar, Pants on Fire* both relate to the theme of honesty and integrity. Courage is the theme of Susanna Pitzer's *Not Afraid of Dogs* and Patricia Polacco's *The Butterfly*. Determination and perseverance are shown in Kathleen Krull's biographies *Wilma Unlimited* and *The Boy Who Invented TV*.

Following are common themes in stories, biographies, plays, and poems. Look at what you plan to have your students read, and decide which of your stories, biographies, plays, or poems relate to these themes. Add any other themes you can think of to the list.

TIP

You can use Themes, Morals, and Lessons Learned with all elementary students as long as you choose stories that are appropriate for the grade you teach.

- Courage and bravery
- Honesty and integrity
- Determination and perseverance
- Hope and optimism
- Generosity and unselfishness
- Creativity
- Curiosity

- Tolerance and open-mindedness
- Fairness and justice
- Prudence and wisdom
- Zest and enthusiasm
- Kindness and compassion
- Individuality and uniqueness

Using the gradual release of responsibility model of instruction, Themes, Morals, and Lessons Learned combines student trios and teacher-led collaborative conversations to discuss various aspects of a text's content.

A Sample Themes, Morals, and Lessons Learned Lesson: Part One

This is the first Themes, Morals, and Lessons Learned lesson Mrs. M.'s class has experienced. The lesson takes place across several days. She splits the lesson into two parts. First, she focuses students' attention on who, when, and where questions. Next, students reread the text and focus on what they can learn from it. Mrs. M. decides to focus this first lesson on determination and perseverance and has chosen four biographies in which the main character clearly shows these character traits.

Purpose Setting

To introduce characters, settings, and events, Mrs. M. uses a simple story map. (See figure 5.1.) She displays this map and makes sure students understand all the terms. When she gets to the last line—*themes, morals, and lessons learned*—she tells students that today they are going to focus on who, when, and where. Tomorrow, they will think about what they can learn from the story.

Main Characters:

Setting (Time and Place):

Problem or Goal:

Major Events:

Themes, Morals, and Lessons Learned:

Figure 5.1: Story map.

Mrs. M. holds up several biographies and tells students they are first going to work as a whole class to complete the story map for the biography of Wilma Rudolph. (Consider using *Wilma Unlimited*.) Next, they will work together in trios to complete a story map based on one of the other biographies.

I Do, and You Watch

Mrs. M. reads several pages of the biography, stopping periodically to add information to the story map. As she adds information, she thinks aloud, modeling how she knows what to add.

She says, "The story begins when Wilma is born in 1940 in Tennessee, so I know when and where the setting was at the beginning. Wilma is clearly an important character.

"Wilma gets polio, and there is no cure. This is clearly the big problem.

"Here are some events I think are important so far in the story."

As Mrs. M. thinks aloud, she adds information to the map and finishes the "I do, and you watch" phase (see figure 5.2, page 44).

Main Characters:

Wilma Rudolph

Setting (Time and Place):

Tennessee, 1940

Major Events:

Wilma gets polio, and there is no cure for it.

Wilma does leg exercises and gets a leg brace.

Wilma goes to school but can't play basketball with the other kids.

Wilma keeps exercising, and when she is twelve, she can walk without the brace.

Themes, Morals, and Lessons Learned:

Figure 5.2: Sample story map filled in.

TIP

Notice how many of your students are participating during the "I do, and you help" part of the lesson. If five or six of your students are giving all the responses, encourage other students to participate. You may want to move students who sit in the back and don't participate to front-row seats!

TIP

Create trios that contain a variety of abilities. Designate the struggling reader to sit in the middle and hold the book. Have the most fluent writer be the scribe. The students will not catch on to your system, if you occasionally designate a good reader to hold the book and an average writer to be the scribe.

I Do, and You Help

For the second part of the biography, Mrs. M. reads aloud and stops periodically to invite the students to help her add information to the map. They tell her about how Wilma becomes a basketball star and then goes to college on a track-and-field scholarship. She is so good she goes to the Olympics and wins three gold medals.

(See figure 5.3 for a partially completed story map.)

You Do It Together, and I Help

The class quickly gets into trios. Mrs. M. gives one copy of one of the biographies to the student in the middle of the trio so everyone can read the book. She hands one copy of the story map to the most able writer in each trio and asks that student to be the scribe. Students are unaware of how Mrs. M. chooses the scribe, so no negative labeling occurs.

The students eagerly begin to read their biographies and add information to the story map. Mrs. M. circulates, giving help as needed. The biggest problem the students encounter with this first story map is that they want to add every character and event. Mrs. M. guides them to decide which characters played major roles and which events were most important.

Main Characters:

Wilma Rudolph and Tennessee State track-and-field coach

Setting (Time and Place):

Tennessee, 1940, and Rome, 1960

Major Events:

Wilma gets polio, and there is no cure for it.

Wilma does leg exercises and gets a leg brace.

Wilma goes to school but can't play basketball with the other kids.

Wilma keeps exercising, and when she is twelve, she can walk without the brace.

Wilma becomes a basketball star, and her team goes to the state finals. They lose the last game.

Wilma goes to college on a track-and-field scholarship.

Wilma goes to the Olympics and wins three gold medals.

Themes, Morals, and Lessons Learned:

Figure 5.3: Sample story map filled in.

The Class Debriefs

The lesson ends with Mrs. M. having the trios share the information on their story maps. Two or three trios have read the same biography and record similar information on their story maps.

A Sample Themes, Morals, and Lessons Learned Lesson: Part Two

In the second part of the lesson, Mrs. M. shifts students' attention to what they can learn from the biographies. She has chosen the four biographies, because they each emphasize the importance of determination and perseverance.

Purpose Setting and Vocabulary Building

On the following day, Mrs. M. works with the whole class to build the concept of determination and perseverance. She reminds them of a story they are all familiar with: *The Little Engine That Could*. Next, she writes the words *determination* and *perseverance* on index cards, has everyone pronounce these two big words, and says, "You show determination and perseverance when you continue to work at something even when it is hard. It was hard for the little blue engine to pull the toy train over the mountain, but he was determined to do it, and eventually he succeeded. Can you think of anything that was hard for you but you kept working at it until you succeeded?"

The students eagerly share personal memories of learning to ride without training wheels, earning belts in karate, learning to swim, and earning badges in various scout groups.

As each student shares his or her experiences, Mrs. M. points to the words and says, "Even though it was hard, you didn't give up. You were showing determination and perseverance."

I Do, and You Watch

Next, she holds up the four biographies and asks students if they thought Wilma and the person their trio read about had shown determination and perseverance. Everyone agrees, and Mrs. M. tells them that she agrees too but that they need to find evidence to support their opinions.

She says, "I have marked the Wilma biography with five sticky notes, because I think there are five clear examples of Wilma showing determination and perseverance. I am going to read until I get to the first sticky note and then tell you what evidence I found in this part that Wilma was determined and wouldn't give up."

Mrs. M. reads until she gets to the first sticky note, and then she stops and thinks aloud about Wilma and determination and perseverance. She says, "I can tell Wilma was determined to learn to walk, because she practiced her leg exercises constantly, even when it really hurt."

Mrs. M. then reads until she comes to the second sticky note and again explains how Wilma's action lets the class infer that she is a determined person who doesn't give up when things get hard.

"In this part," she says, "she took off her leg brace and walked down the church aisle without it, even though her leg was trembling and really hurt."

I Do, and You Help

She continues, "There are three more sticky notes that mark other clear examples of Wilma's determination and perseverance. When I get to these, I will stop, and you all can help me explain how Wilma showed her determination and perseverance."

Mrs. M. reads until she gets to the remaining three sticky notes, stopping at each one to let students explain what Wilma had done to show determination and perseverance.

One student volunteers, "She learned to play basketball and took her team to the finals of the state championship."

Another says, "When she went to the Olympics in Rome, she won the 100-meter race even though she had twisted her ankle, and it was swollen and painful."

"She got behind in the relay race because she almost dropped the baton, but she ran faster than she ever had and won it by a fraction of a second," says a third student.

You Do It Together, and I Help

Mrs. M. says, "Now, it's your turn to prove that the person you read about showed determination and perseverance. You are going to work in your trios and add sticky notes to mark stopping places where you find clear examples of how the person showed he or she was determined and not going to give up. When we get back together, your trio is going to show where you put the sticky notes and explain your evidence for concluding that your character had determination and perseverance."

The class quickly gets into trios and begins rereading their biographies. Mrs. M. gives each trio five sticky notes and asks students to decide on the five best examples of determination and perseverance and mark those examples with sticky notes. Mrs. M. circulates around the groups, coaching students as necessary to explain their examples.

The Class Debriefs

On the third day, the class begins with the trios finishing their reading and preparing to share examples of determination and perseverance from their biographies. Mrs. M. then gathers the class and lets each trio share one example. The students are clearly pleased to see that other trios found many of the same examples from the biographies they've read.

Next, Mrs. M. goes to the board and says, "I want us to construct some statements showing what we learned about determination and perseverance from reading all these books. I am going to post these statements along with copies of the covers of the books here so that we can remember what we learned."

The first student who raises her hand says, "Wilma showed determination because she didn't give up even when things got tough."

Mrs. M. agrees that this was true about Wilma and asks if any of the people they had read about with their trios had also not given up when the going got tough or when others thought they couldn't do something. The students eagerly share examples, and then Mrs. M. helps them construct a statement about determination that is not tied to any one person.

She writes: "You can do things no one thought you could do, if you show determination and perseverance and don't give up."

The discussion continues, and as students share specific examples, Mrs. M. broadens them to include others. It is difficult for many students to move to this abstract level of thinking, but Mrs. M. leads them with determination and perseverance until the

TIP

The perfect time to use formative assessment and listen in on trios' thinking is when they are working together.

class constructs three more statements of lessons they learned. She writes the following statements on the board.

- *Sometimes, if you don't succeed the first time, and you keep trying and don't give up, you can eventually do it.*
- *Determination means you really want to do something, and perseverance means you keep trying until you do.*
- *Most famous people have problems and failures, but they show determination and persevere until they succeed.*

Suddenly, a student has an aha moment and says, "I know what my dad would say about this. He would say, 'If at first you don't succeed, try, try again.' My dad is always saying corny things like that!"

Mrs. M. declares his dad is a very wise man and adds this to the other statements on the board. In the coming days, she uses these to encourage students when they encounter a difficult task or give up after failing at something the first time.

She realizes that an unintended consequence of these lessons is that some students are now trying harder. She ponders which character trait she could work on next that would both help students achieve the standard of inferring themes, morals, and lessons learned and move them forward in their own character development.

Planning and Teaching a Themes, Morals, and Lessons Learned Lesson

The key to success with a Themes, Morals, and Lessons Learned lesson is to choose texts with characters who clearly demonstrate the trait you are focusing on. For the first part of the lesson, decide on the text to use for your read-aloud and the "I do, and you watch" and "I do, and you help" phases. Choose a story map format that works for your class. We've offered one option, but you can alter it to meet your class's needs. For the second part of the lesson, use sticky notes to mark stopping points where a character does something that clearly demonstrates the trait. Use the following nine steps when teaching a Themes, Morals, and Lessons Learned lesson.

1. Read aloud one of the texts you have chosen. Use the "I do, and you watch" and "I do, and you help" phases to record information about characters, settings, and events on a story map.

2. Put students in trios, including at least one good and one struggling reader. Give each trio one copy of a book and one copy of the blank story map. Depending on your resources, the trios can all be reading the same book, or they can have three or four different titles, with two or three trios reading each title. Have them complete the story map. Circulate and help students decide which characters and events are important for them to include.

3. Have trios share their story maps with the class.

4. When students have determined important elements from the text, shift their attention to the themes, morals, and lessons they learned. Have students share personal experiences and connect the words to those experiences. For example, for bravery and courage, ask, "Who is the bravest person you know? How did he or she demonstrate bravery? When have you been brave? Does being brave mean you aren't afraid? Are courage and bravery similar? When have you shown courage? When has someone you know shown courage? What characters in books and videos have been especially brave and courageous? What did they do to let you know that?"

5. Use sticky notes to flag places in the text when a character demonstrates the specific trait. Read the text again to your students, stopping at the first sticky note and modeling why you think this action shows that the person demonstrates the concept. For example, say, "I think Branch Rickey was very courageous when he hired Jackie Robinson to be the first black baseball player in the major league. He knew many people were going to think he should never have put an African American on the team, but he did it anyway because it was the right thing to do." Model two more examples, explaining how the character's action demonstrates the concept.

6. After letting students watch you think aloud about a few examples, ask students for their help. Say, "I am going to read to the next sticky note. When I stop, I want you to help me decide who was showing _____ and what this person did to demonstrate it." Finish the book, stopping at the remaining sticky notes and using the "I do, and you help" phase.

7. Have students get into their trios. Give them four to six sticky notes, and ask them to read until they find a clear example of the concept. Have them place a sticky note to mark each example and discuss what the character does to demonstrate the concept. Circulate among your students, and be sure all trios are supporting their decisions with evidence from the text during this "You do it together, and I help" phase.

8. Gather your students, and have the trios share examples of characters demonstrating the concept. Help them share their thinking by asking, "How does _____ show that this person was _____?" If students have been reading different texts, have the trios that read each text present their examples and evidence together.

9. Using examples from all books the students read and your read-aloud, ask students what they have learned about the specific trait. Ask, "What is the lesson we can learn about _____ from all these books?" Record several examples so students see there is not just one right answer.

Themes, Morals, and Lessons Learned Lessons Across the Year

In subsequent lessons, as students demonstrate their ability to determine what characters' actions tell us about them, ask the trios, "What is the lesson we can learn from reading this book?" before assembling the class for sharing. Have trios share examples of the concept, cite evidence, and offer their lesson learned with the whole class. When your observations of the group interactions in the trios indicate that most of your students have learned to infer character traits from actions and construct statements of lessons learned, give them a text to read and a trait to focus on, and have them complete the task independently ("You do, and I watch"). Don't be surprised if students require lots of work with this lesson framework before they achieve independence. Determining the theme, moral, or lesson learned requires an exceptionally high level of abstract thinking.

Your students need to learn to think about what they can learn from stories when reading on their own. Once you have done several Themes, Morals, and Lessons Learned lessons, notice which students have chosen to read stories and chapter books for independent reading time. When the independent reading time is over, ask these students if they think what they were reading has a theme, moral, or lesson. Let students tell what the theme, moral, or lesson is and share examples from the text to support their ideas.

How Themes, Morals, and Lessons Learned Lessons Teach the Standards

Themes, Morals, and Lessons Learned lessons teach Reading anchor standard one (CCRA.R.1) because students learn to make logical inferences about character actions and traits and to cite textual evidence to support these inferences. Creating the story map focuses student attention on important characters, settings, and events in narratives and thus helps you teach Reading anchor standard three (CCRA.R.3). The major emphasis in Themes, Morals, and Lessons Learned is teaching students how to determine the theme, moral, or lesson learned from a story, poem, or play, which is a major focus of Reading anchor standard two (CCRA.R.2). The lessons teach Speaking and Listening anchor standard one (CCRA.SL.1) as well, because students participate in collaborative conversations while working in trios and with the whole class.

CCSS in a Main Idea Tree Lesson

Main Idea Tree is a lesson framework to teach students how to organize and summarize informational text. When you lead students through this lesson, you are helping them learn the reading, writing, and speaking and listening skills in the following standards.

Reading
RI.1.2: Identify the main idea, and retell key details of a text.

RI.2.2: Identify the main topic of a multiparagraph text as well as the focus of specific paragraphs within the text.

RI.3.2: Determine the main idea of a text; recount the key details, and explain how they support the main idea.

RI.4.2: Determine the main idea of a text, and explain how it is supported by key details; summarize the text.

RI.5.2: Determine two or more main ideas of a text, and explain how they are supported by key details; summarize the text.

Writing
CCRA.W.2: Write informative/explanatory texts to examine and convey complex ideas and information clearly and accurately through the effective selection, organization, and analysis of content.

CCRA.W.10: Write routinely over extended time frames (time for research, reflection, and revision) and shorter time frames (a single sitting or a day or two) for a range of tasks, purposes, and audiences.

Speaking and Listening
CCRA.SL.1: Prepare for and participate effectively in a range of conversations and collaborations with diverse partners, building on others' ideas and expressing their own clearly and persuasively.

Source: Adapted from NGA & CCSSO, 2010, pp. 13–14, 18, 22.

CHAPTER 6

Main Idea Tree

Informational text often includes several main ideas about a single topic. A Main Idea Tree lesson can help students visualize and organize information. The trunk of the tree symbolizes the topic you are learning about. The large branches hold the main ideas, and smaller branches hold any details that relate to them. The major focus of a Main Idea Tree lesson is to help students determine main ideas in informational texts and write summaries that include supporting details. Using the gradual release of responsibility model of instruction, the Main Idea Tree lesson framework combines student trios and teacher-led collaborative conversations to discuss various aspects of the text's content. In part one of the lesson, students record main ideas and key details on their trees. In part two of the lesson, they learn to write summaries by referring to the information recorded on their trees. The major focus of a Main Idea Tree lesson is to help students determine main ideas in informational texts and write summaries that include supporting details. Using the gradual release of responsibility model of instruction, the Main Idea Tree lesson framework combines student trios and teacher-led collaborative conversations to discuss various aspects of the text's content.

A Sample Main Idea Tree Lesson: Part One

The students in this class have shown in other lessons that they are confused about the difference between main ideas and details and with summarizing informational text. Mr. S. has chosen to use the Main Idea Tree lesson framework to help students see that main ideas are like the big, main branches of the tree and that the details are the smaller branches that connect to the main branches. Once students organize information on the tree's branches, he will use this structure to help them learn to write paragraph summaries with topic sentences and supporting details.

TIP

Students can learn to construct a Main Idea Tree and write simple summaries starting in the spring of grade 1.

Purpose Setting

Mr. S.'s class is going to read an informational article about snakes. He realizes that this piece of descriptive text has several main ideas about snakes with details to support each idea. He decides to help students visualize the main ideas and details by having them draw a tree and put main ideas on the large branches of the tree and details on small branches.

Mr. S. puts a large sheet of paper on the board and draws a large tree with six big branches. He labels the trunk with the word *topic* and the branches with *main idea*.

He says, "Often when we are reading informational text, we are learning a lot of big ideas about one topic. We call these big, important ideas *main ideas*. Today, we are going to be reading about snakes. We are going to create trees and write the big ideas we learn about snakes on the big branches. Then, we are going to draw some smaller branches and write details that tell more about the main ideas." Mr. S. writes the word *detail* on the smaller branches. (See figure 6.1.)

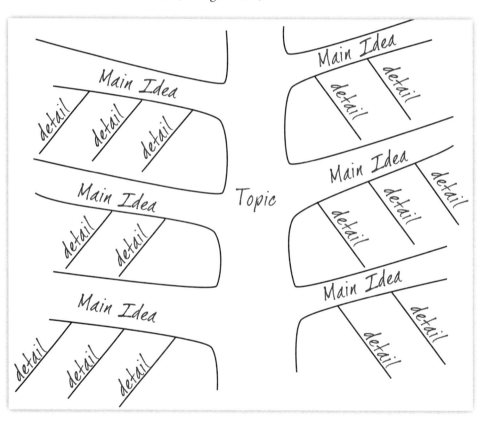

Figure 6.1: Sample Main Idea Tree.

TIP

Have students draw their own tree rather than handing out a copy with an already drawn tree. Your goal is for students to construct this tree in their minds whenever they read descriptive text with several main ideas. Many students like to draw and thus will be more engaged in the lesson!

Mr. S. gives everyone a large piece of drawing paper.

"Use the whole paper," he says, "so you will have lots of space to draw smaller branches and write the details. Instead of the word *topic*, write *snakes* on the trunk."

Students eagerly draw their trees, and Mr. S. sees they are intrigued with the idea of creating their snake trees.

I Do, and You Watch

When all students have drawn their trees and have written the word *snakes* on the trunk, Mr. S. reads to them the first section of the text that describes snakes' bodies. When he finishes reading this section, he thinks aloud, saying, "I learned a lot of facts about snakes on this page. I learned that they don't have any arms or legs. They have eyes on the sides of their heads and really long bellies. Their skin is scaly and dry. I think this section is all about snakes' bodies, so I am going to write that on one of my tree branches. Then, I am going to draw some smaller branches off the main branch and write the details I learned about their bodies."

Mr. S. writes this main idea and its details on one branch of the tree. His students copy this information on one of their tree branches. (See figure 6.2.)

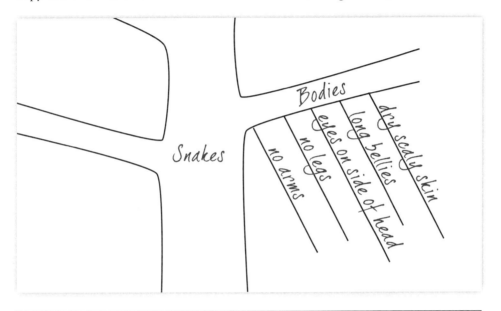

Figure 6.2: Sample Main Idea Tree with details about snakes.

I Do, and You Help

Mr. S. says, "Now, we are going to read the next section together. Get in your trios, and I will give you one copy of the article. Remember that the person I hand the article to needs to sit in the middle and hold the text so that everyone can read it."

"After we read it, we will talk about what we learned and come up with a main idea that relates to all the details," he continues.

Mr. S. and the students read the section chorally. When they finish, he asks the students what they learned.

One student says, "Snakes shed their skins two or three times every year."

Another chimes in, saying, "The old skin wears out and just peels off."

A third says, "There is a new skin that grew under the old skin."

Mr. S. then leads students to determine the main idea of this section, saying, "So, these details are all about one idea. Who can tell us what all these details are about? What is the main idea of this section?"

TIP

Students work together and interact more when they have just one copy of the text. Handing the text to a struggling reader increases the chance that the student will actively participate, and holding the text confers status on that student!

TIP

Notice how many of your students are participating during the "I do, and you help" part of the lesson. If five or six of your students are giving all the responses, encourage other students to participate. You may want to make a list of your students and check off the ones who responded for several lessons. If this formative assessment tells you that some students are consistently not engaged, call on them first in subsequent lessons.

The class decides that this section is all about how snakes shed their skins. Mr. S. and the students all write this on a branch, and they draw smaller branches to write the details about how snakes shed their skins. (See figure 6.3.)

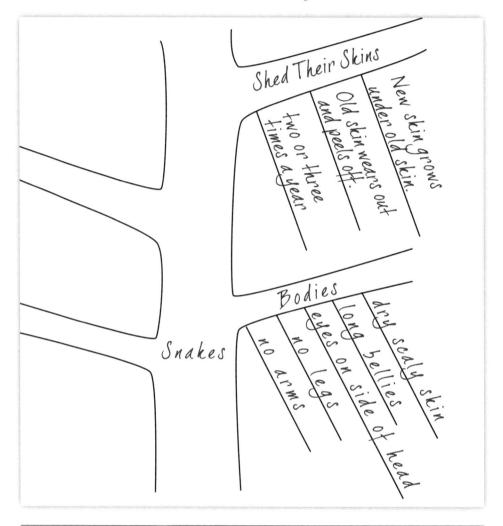

Figure 6.3: Sample Main Idea Tree with details about snakes.

You Do It Together, and I Help

Mr. S. says, "Now it is time to work with your friends and finish the snake tree. You will start reading on this page where we left off. I have put these small sticky notes at each stopping point. When you get to the sticky note, stop and tell each other what you learned. Then, come up with a main idea that all the details relate to. Write the main idea and details on your tree before going on to the next section."

As his students work together, Mr. S. circulates among them and observes the interactions of the groups. The students are all able to tell the details, but some groups have difficulty coming up with the main idea, and Mr. S. helps them.

He notes, "You learned that a thread snake can be the size of a worm and an anaconda can be as long as a bus, cobras can be eight to eighteen feet, and garter snakes are usually one to four feet. What's the big idea about snakes we learn from thinking about those sizes?"

One student smiles and responds in a questioning tone: "Snakes are different sizes?"

Mr. S. says, "Exactly," and the students write this main idea and the details on a branch of their trees.

The trios finish at different times, and Mr. S. encourages students to turn their papers over and draw some of what they learned about snakes to keep them engaged while others are still working. When the slower groups see the others drawing, they pick up the pace and quickly complete their trees. (See figure 6.5 for a sample completed Main Idea Tree.)

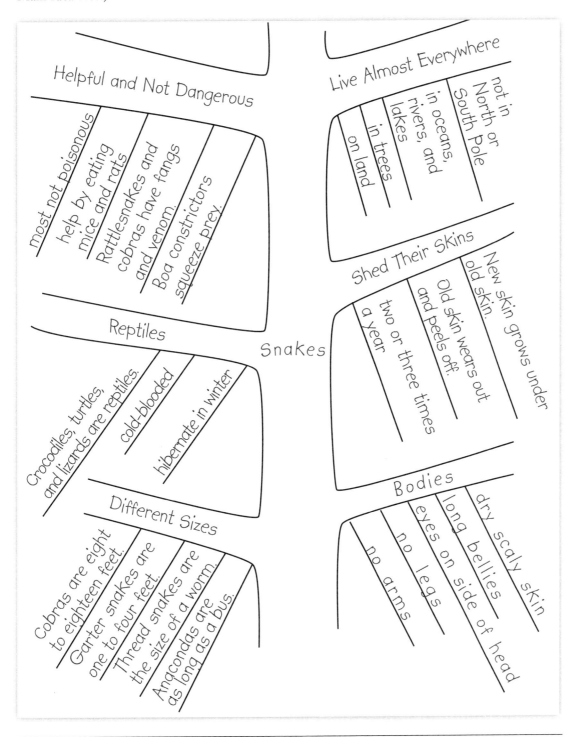

Figure 6.5: Sample completed Main Idea Tree.

The Class Debriefs

When students have completed their trees, Mr. S. gathers them, and they compare what they have written. They notice that although the wording of the main ideas and details vary, almost all the trees have the same ideas on the branches. The students are clearly proud of their trees. Mr. S. tells them they will need their trees tomorrow to help them construct summaries, and when the summaries are done, they can take their trees home and tell their families all the big ideas and details they learned about snakes.

A Sample Main Idea Tree Lesson: Part Two

On the following day, Mr. S. extends the Main Idea Tree lesson to help students learn to write summaries. He brings out his tree, which has only two branches complete. Students share what they have written on the other four branches, and he completes his tree. The wording of the main ideas and details vary slightly from group to group. Mr. S. assures the students that there are different ways to word these ideas and that all their main ideas and details are correct.

I Do, and You Watch

"Now, we are going to write summaries telling everything we learned about snakes," Mr. S. says. "Our snake tree has six big branches, and we are going to write a paragraph for each branch. I am going to write the first one, and you are going to help me write the second one. Then, you are going to get in your trios and write one together. That will leave three main ideas that you'll need to summarize. Each of you will write a paragraph summarizing one of the remaining three branches."

Mr. S. looks at all six branches and then writes "Snakes are reptiles" on the board.

He says, "Which main idea branch have I chosen to write about? That's right. The main idea is reptiles, so I just turned that into a sentence to start my paragraph. Now I will add the details about reptiles."

Mr. S. then reads all the details on the *reptiles* branch: "cold-blooded, hibernate in winter, and crocodiles, turtles, and lizards."

"I am going to add these details to my paragraph," he says, "but I need to turn them into sentences and explain a little more about them. I am going to tell that reptiles are cold-blooded and explain what that means."

Mr. S. adds two sentences to the paragraph: "Reptiles are cold-blooded animals. The body temperature of cold-blooded animals stays the same as the air temperature."

Mr. S. completes the paragraph with sentences explaining the other two details.

> Snakes are reptiles. Reptiles are cold-blooded animals. The body temperature of cold-blooded animals stays the same as the air temperature. If they live in cold places, they hibernate in the winter to stay warm. Other reptiles include crocodiles, lizards, and turtles.

I Do, and You Help

He continues by saying, "Now, we are going to construct the next paragraph together. I want to write the next paragraph about this main idea."

Mr. S. points to the *different sizes* branch and asks, "Who can help me put this idea into a sentence?"

The class decides that the first sentence should be: "Snakes are many different sizes."

Students then help him put the details into sentences, and jointly, the class constructs a paragraph.

Snakes are many different sizes. A thread snake is only as big as a worm. Garter snakes are usually one to four feet long, but cobras can be eight to eighteen feet long. An anaconda can be as long as a bus.

You Do It Together, and I Help

Having watched and then helped Mr. S. construct two paragraphs, the students are eager to construct their own paragraphs. They quickly assemble into their trios and choose one of the main ideas to work on together. Mr. S. circulates among his students and assists, but most trios have no difficulty constructing the paragraphs. Finally, they divide the remaining three paragraphs among themselves, and each student writes a paragraph. One trio has trouble deciding who will write which one.

Mr. S. says, "If you can't decide, I will decide for you."

As Mr. S. suspected, the students quickly make the decision themselves. Mr. S. knows who is apt to have trouble getting started on the individual paragraphs and moves around helping those students formulate a first sentence if they need this help.

The Class Debriefs

To conclude the lesson, Mr. S. has the students stand in a big circle around the room. He lets volunteers read the paragraphs they have written individually.

Planning and Teaching a Main Idea Tree Lesson

The crucial part of planning a Main Idea Tree lesson is selecting the right text. Look for an informational piece about one topic that has several big ideas. This kind of text is often called descriptive text. Two other text structures that you will commonly find in elementary informational texts are sequential (or causal) and comparative. (Chapters 7 and 8, pages 63 and 73, describe lesson frameworks for these informational text structures.)

Once you have chosen the text, decide how many main ideas about the topic the text includes, and determine stopping points to focus students' attention on one main idea at a time. Put sticky notes at each stopping point on the texts the trios will read. Use the following six steps when teaching a Main Idea Tree lesson.

1. Set the purpose for the lesson. On a large piece of paper, draw a tree with five or six branches. Label the trunk with the word *topic* and the big branches with the phrase *main idea*. Explain to students that when you read about an informational topic, you often learn many important ideas about one topic. Tell students that when you read information that describes one topic, you can organize that information like a tree. Tell them that they are going to learn to construct trees and put the main ideas on big branches and supporting details about the main idea on smaller branches.

2. Give students a large sheet of paper, and have them draw a tree with five or six branches. Have them label the trunk with the topic they are reading about.

3. Model how to formulate a main idea by reading the first section of the text aloud to the students and talking about what details you learned. Formulate and write a main idea on one of the big branches, and draw smaller branches to write the details. Let all students copy the main idea and details on their trees.

4. Arrange students into trios, including an advanced and struggling reader in each trio. Give one student a copy of the text, and ask that student to sit between the other two. Have students read the second section with you, and ask them to tell you what details they learned. Have them help you construct the main idea. Write this main idea and details on a second branch, and have students record this information on their trees.

5. Tell students that they are going to read together to complete their trees. Have them identify stopping points that you have marked with sticky notes. Circulate and give help as needed. Make sure that students are stopping at the appropriate places and completing each main branch of the tree before they continue reading.

6. In part two of the lesson, teach students how to write summary paragraphs. Model how to turn one of the main idea branches into a paragraph with a main idea sentence and supporting details. Let students help you construct a paragraph for a second branch. Have students work together and then individually write paragraphs for the remaining branches.

Main Idea Tree Lessons Across the Year

In subsequent lessons, as students demonstrate their ability to determine main ideas and details, gradually fade out the modeling and helping steps, and let the trios construct trees for the entire text. Similarly, as students learn how to construct summary paragraphs based on main ideas, fade out the modeling and helping steps in writing the paragraphs. When your formative assessments indicate that most of your students can determine main ideas and associated details, have them construct a Main Idea Tree and write a summary paragraph independently ("You do, and I watch"). Don't be surprised if students require lots of work with this lesson framework before they achieve independence. Recording details is a fairly simple process, but formulating a main idea requires a high level of thinking and lots of practice.

To help students apply their main idea skills when reading on their own, observe what your students are reading during their independent reading time. For students who are reading an informational text with several big ideas about one topic, suggest that they construct a tree to show the main ideas and details. Let students who decide to construct trees share them with the class.

How Main Idea Tree Lessons Teach the Standards

Main Idea Tree lessons teach students to determine main ideas and key details and summarize what they learned, which is the major focus for Reading informational text standard two (RI.2). Writing summaries based on the information recorded on the tree helps students learn to write informative and explanatory text, as required in Writing anchor standard two (CCRA.W.2). The lesson teaches Writing anchor standard ten (CCRA.W.10), because the pieces students produce make a contribution to the routine writing the Common Core expects all students to do. When students work together to complete the trees, they are talking with each other and thus moving toward meeting Speaking and Listening anchor standard one (CCRA.SL.1).

CCSS in a Sequence / Cause and Effect Lesson

Sequence / Cause and Effect lessons help students organize information from informational text. When you lead students through this lesson several times and gradually release responsibility to them, you are helping them learn the reading, writing, and speaking and listening skills in the following standards.

Reading

RI.2.3: Describe the connection between a series of historical events, scientific ideas or concepts, or steps in technical procedures in a text.

RI.3.3: Describe the relationship between a series of historical events, scientific ideas or concepts, or steps in technical procedures in a text, using language that pertains to time, sequence, and cause and effect.

RI.4.3: Explain events, procedures, ideas, or concepts in a historical, scientific, or technical text, including what happened and why, based on specific information in the text.

Writing

CCRA.W.2: Write informative/explanatory texts to examine and convey complex ideas and information clearly and accurately through the effective selection, organization, and analysis of content.

Speaking and Listening

CCRA.SL.1: Prepare for and participate effectively in a range of conversations and collaborations with diverse partners, building on others' ideas and expressing their own clearly and persuasively.

Source: Adapted from NGA & CCSSO, 2010, pp. 13–14, 18, 22.

CHAPTER 7

Sequence / Cause and Effect

There are three common text structures found in informational text. First, many texts are descriptive. These texts focus on a single topic and present important facts about that topic. Main Idea Tree lessons (chapter 6, page 53) help readers organize ideas from descriptive informational texts. Second, some informational texts compare and contrast various items in a category. Double bubbles and data charts (chapter 8, page 73) help students compare and contrast two or more items to organize information from an informational text. The third common text structure organizes ideas or events according to the order in which they occur. Sometimes one event causes another event, and there is a sequential relationship and a cause-and-effect relationship between events. Reading informational text standard three (RI.3) requires students to understand these sequence and cause-and-effect relationships. Timelines and step maps are organizing frameworks that help students think about and describe these relationships. Once students record the order of events, they decide if any of the events caused other events. Constructing timelines and step maps helps focus student attention on these important sequential and causal relationships.

The major focus of Sequence / Cause and Effect lessons is to help students determine sequence and causal effects while reading and write summaries of those relationships. The lesson framework focuses on two lessons: creating timelines and constructing step maps. Using the gradual release of responsibility model of instruction, Sequence / Cause and Effect combines student trios and teacher-led collaborative conversations to discuss various aspects of the text's content.

A Sample Sequence / Cause and Effect Lesson: Timelines

In their daily life, most elementary students understand sequence and cause-and-effect relationships. In this example, Mr. T. and students chart their daily activities in the classroom on a timeline. For homework, students chart their individual activities from the time they leave school through the rest of the day.

TIP

Sequence / Cause and Effect lessons can be used from kindergarten on as long as you choose text that is appropriate for the grade you teach.

Purpose Setting

Mr. T. begins the day by gathering the students and drawing a long vertical line on the board. He labels the timeline with the date and adds the first entry: "8:43 a.m.—Read-aloud."

"Today," he tells the class, "we are going to record every activity we do and the time we begin that activity. We will be creating a timeline of our school day. For homework tonight, I am going to give you all a copy of our class timeline, and you are going to finish it by adding the activities you do and the times you do them once you leave the classroom for the rest of the day."

Mr. T. then reads to the class from a biography of Neil Armstrong. When he finishes the read-aloud, he asks the students what they will be doing next, and they add "9:03 a.m.—Math stations" to the timeline and proceed to this activity. Throughout the day, Mr. T. and his students record both scheduled (lunch, science, and pack-up) and unexpected events (rain shower and indoor recess) to their timelines.

At the end of the day, Mr. T. and his students review the events, and then Mr. T. asks if any of the events caused other events. It takes some prompting, but the students soon see that the sudden rain shower caused them to have indoor recess. Mr. T. draws an arrow from *rain shower* to *indoor recess* and explains, "Many of the events in our day just follow one another. But sometimes, an event happens that causes another event to happen. That happened today when it started to rain just as we were heading to the playground, and we had recess indoors instead of outdoors. I drew this arrow to show that one event caused another event. We had indoor recess because of the rain. The rain was the cause and indoor recess was the effect, and we use an arrow to show that. You are going to complete this timeline for yourself once you leave the classroom. If anything happens that causes another thing to happen, draw an arrow from the cause to the effect." (See figure 7.1 for Mr. T.'s timeline.)

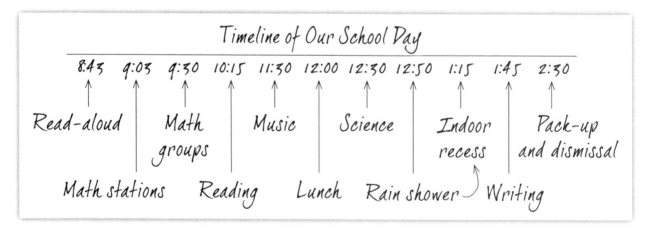

Figure 7.1: Sample timeline.

The next morning, the students eagerly share their timelines. Most recorded every event and precise times. It was clear students enjoyed charting their activities. Several students had arrows between events, and everyone listened intently as one student explained that yelling at his little brother caused him to have fifteen minutes of time-out, and another explained that missing the soccer kick caused his team to lose the game.

Mr. T. tells his students, "We can make timelines to document sequence and cause-and-effect relationships in things we read about. Today, we are going to read an article from our student magazine about the history of space exploration. We are going to record important dates and events on our timeline. If we decide that any event caused another event to happen, we will draw an arrow just like we did to show cause-and-effect relationships in our day."

Mr. T. draws a long vertical line and labels the timeline "Space Exploration" (see figure 7.2).

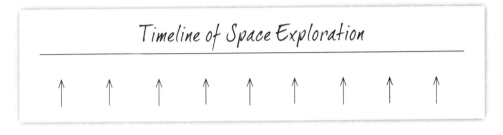

Figure 7.2: Sample timeline of space exploration.

I Do, and You Watch

He says, "I am going to read the first part of this article to you and show you what I think are important dates and events."

After reading the first three paragraphs, Mr. T. begins the timeline and adds the following dates and events. (See figure 7.3.)

- **1947:** Fruit flies were the first animals ever launched into space.

- **1949:** Albert, a rhesus monkey, was launched into space.

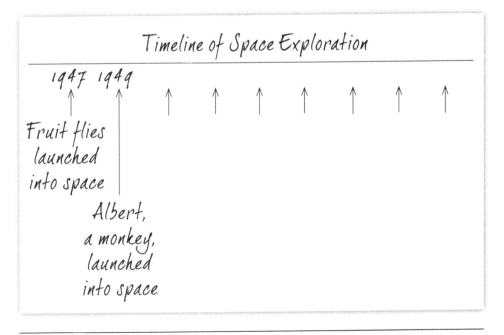

Figure 7.3: Sample timeline of space exploration with key dates and events.

The students are all amazed that fruit flies were the first animals in space, and a lively discussion ensues about why fruit flies were chosen. Mr. T. tells them that that would be a good question for someone to research and find an explanation. He then explains that the reason he chose to put these two events on the timeline was that before these events, no living creatures had ever gone into space.

I Do, and You Help

Before reading the next section to his students, Mr. T. tells them that they are going to help him record the next few events on the timeline. He reads four paragraphs, and students decide to add the following events.

- **1957:** Russia launched Sputnik 1, the first satellite ever to orbit Earth.
- **1957:** Russia launched Sputnik 2 with a dog named Laika, the first animal ever to orbit Earth.
- **1961:** Russian astronaut Yuri Gagarin was the first human to orbit Earth.
- **1963:** President John F. Kennedy declared America would be first to get to the moon, and the Space Race began.

When Mr. T. records the 1963 entry, he asks students what they think caused President Kennedy to say America would be the first country to the moon. Someone suggests that it was because the Russians had been first to orbit Earth, and we wanted to beat the Russians to the moon. Mr. T. helps the students see the cause-and-effect relationship between Russia and America and draws an arrow between these two events. (See figure 7.4.)

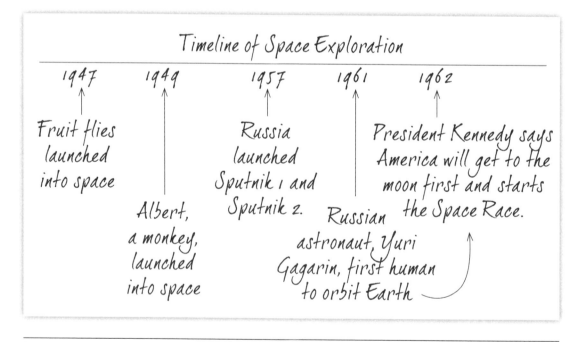

Figure 7.4: Sample timeline with events and arrow.

You Do It Together, and I Help

"Now it's your turn to finish the timeline," Mr. T. announces.

The prearranged trios assemble, and Mr. T. gives one person in each trio a copy of the article and designates another person to be the scribe.

The students eagerly read and complete the timeline. One trio realizes that the 1986 explosion of the *Challenger* and the death of all seven astronauts was the cause for the halt in space shuttle exploration for three years. After checking this inference out with Mr. T., the students in this trio proudly draw an arrow between these events to show a cause-and-effect relationship. Mr. T. and the rest of the class are impressed, and Mr. T. knows they will all be thinking harder to find possible causal relationships the next time they construct a timeline.

Once students organize the information about space exploration on a timeline, creating a class summary is the next step. Mr. T. models this by writing an initial paragraph elaborating on the first two entries.

> In 1947, the first animals were launched into space. These animals were fruit flies. When they returned from their quick trip, scientists studied the effects of the flight on their bodies. The next animal to make the trip was a rhesus monkey named Albert. Russia launched him into space in 1949. He flew eighty-three miles from Earth.

Trios work on the remaining events and create a class summary of space exploration.

The Class Debriefs

When the students have finished writing, Mr. T. gathers them together to share their paragraphs.

A Sample Sequence / Cause and Effect Lesson: Step Maps

In addition to following the sequence of events, students need to learn to pay attention to sequence when reading text that explains how to do something. In this part of the sample lesson, Mr. T. and his students work together in the "I do, and you watch" and "I do, and you help" phases of the lesson, and the students work in trios to complete a step map for a specific text.

Purpose Setting

Mr. T. draws a simple step map and labels it "Making a Peanut Butter and Jelly Sandwich for Lunch."

He says, "When we are learning to do something and reading about how to do something, we have to pay attention to all the steps and get them in the right order. Most of you know that many days, I bring a peanut butter and jelly sandwich for lunch. I have

TIP

Include in each trio one of your struggling readers. Hand the book to that struggling reader, and he or she will have an important role in the group. Choose the most fluent writer to do the writing so that it doesn't slow down the reading too much.

TIP

The perfect time to use formative assessment and listen in on trios' thinking is when they are working together.

liked these sandwiches since I was a little kid, and I still do. I am going to show you how I make the sandwich, and then we are going to record all the steps on this step map."

I Do, and You Watch

Mr. T. takes out two slices of bread from a bag, a jar of peanut butter, a jar of jelly, a knife, and a box of sandwich bags. Without saying a word, Mr. T. proceeds to make the sandwich as if he is at home preparing it to take to school.

The students watch intently, and when he finishes, he says, "I am going to write the first two steps on the map, and you are going to help me write the rest of them."

He writes two steps on the map: "Before I can start putting the sandwich together, I like to make sure I have everything ready, so these are the first two steps I do." (See figure 7.5.)

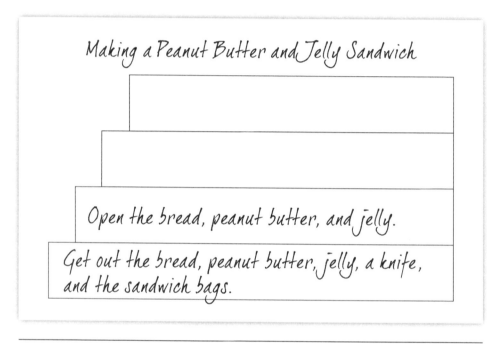

Figure 7.5: Sample step map about making a peanut butter and jelly sandwich.

I Do, and You Help

He then asks the students what he did next, and students help him complete the step map for this simple task.

You Do It Together, and I Help

"Now I have a short story for you to read," Mr. T. says. "In this story, a boy is riding his bike and gets a flat tire. A girl comes out of the house and sees the boy and repairs the tire for him. Your job is to record all the steps you would need to do to repair a flat tire on a bike."

The students quickly get into their assigned trios, read the text, and construct the step map. Mr. T. circulates, watches, and coaches. When he sees several trios forgetting important steps, he reminds them of what he had to do before starting to make the sandwich. (See figure 7.6 for the completed step map.)

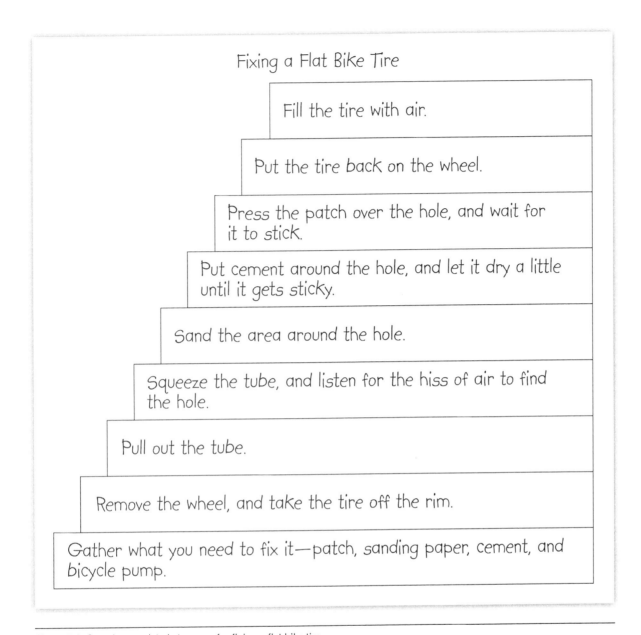

Figure 7.6: Sample completed step map for fixing a flat bike tire.

The Class Debriefs

When students complete their step maps, he gathers them together and lets volunteers share their step maps.

Planning and Teaching a Sequence / Cause and Effect Lesson

The most important consideration in planning a Sequence / Cause and Effect lesson is choosing a text that has an evident sequence of events. When possible, for a lesson in which you are going to have students organize events on a timeline, choose a text in which some of the events cause other events. Students need to learn that sometimes events just follow one another, but other times, an event causes one or more of the events that follow. When organizing events on a timeline, decide the time increments.

The daily schedule example was organized according to time. Students used the year to show the sequence of events in space exploration. Sometimes, *first, second, third,* and *finally* are appropriate transition words with which to organize events to show the sequence.

Use the following seven steps when teaching a Sequence / Cause and Effect lesson.

1. For the first timeline or step map lesson, use a real-life example that shows the importance of sequence and cause-and-effect relationships in your students' lives.

2. Once students understand how a timeline or step map shows sequence and cause-and-effect relationships in the real world, help them transfer this ability to text. Set the purpose for the lesson by telling students that when they are reading, they often need to pay attention to the order in which things happen and decide if some events caused other events.

3. Use the "I do, and you watch" and "I do, and you help" procedures to demonstrate how you can use timelines or step maps to show sequence and cause-and-effect relationships.

4. Organize trios with students of different reading and writing abilities. Give trios one copy of the text, and designate who will do the writing and who will sit in the middle and hold the text.

5. Have students work together to complete a timeline or step map.

6. Circulate, coach, and formatively assess how the groups are interacting and how well they are able to determine sequence and cause-and-effect relationships.

7. Teach students to write summaries in which they use sequence and cause-and-effect words (*first, next, last, finally, therefore, because,* and so on) to show these relationships.

Sequence / Cause and Effect Lessons Across the Year

In subsequent lessons, as students demonstrate their ability to determine sequence and causal relationships, gradually fade out the modeling and helping steps, and let trios construct timelines or step maps for the entire text. Similarly, as students learn how to construct summary paragraphs based on sequence, fade out the modeling and helping steps in writing the paragraphs. When your formative assessment of students in their trios indicates that most can determine sequence and causal relationships, have them construct a timeline or step map and write a summary paragraph independently ("You do, and I watch").

To help students apply their sequence and cause-and-effect skills when reading on their own, observe what your students are reading during their independent reading time. For students who are reading an informational text in which sequence is important, suggest that they construct a timeline or step map to organize the important facts. Let students who decide to construct these share them with the class.

How Sequence / Cause and Effect Lessons Teach the Standards

Sequence / Cause and Effect lessons teach students to determine sequence and causal events while reading and to write summaries that specify sequence and causal relationships, which are focuses for Reading informational text standard three (RI.3). Writing summaries based on information helps students learn to write informative and explanatory text, as Writing anchor standard two (CCRA.W.2) requires. When students work together to create the step maps, they move toward meeting Speaking and Listening anchor standard one (CCRA.SL.1).

CCSS in a Compare and Contrast Lesson

Compare and Contrast is a lesson framework to teach students how to organize similarities and differences in texts. When you lead students through this lesson several times and gradually release responsibility to them, you are helping them learn the reading, writing, and speaking and listening skills in the following standards.

Reading

CCRA.R.9: Analyze how two or more texts address similar themes or topics in order to build knowledge or to compare the approaches the authors take.

RL.5.3: Compare and contrast two or more characters, settings, or events in a story or drama, drawing on specific details in the text (such as how characters interact).

Writing

CCRA.W.2: Write informative/explanatory texts to examine and convey complex ideas and information clearly and accurately through the effective selection, organization, and analysis of content.

CCRA.W.10: Write routinely over extended time frames (time for research, reflection, and revision) and shorter time frames (a single sitting or a day or two) for a range of tasks, purposes, and audiences.

Speaking and Listening

CCRA.SL.1: Prepare for and participate effectively in a range of conversations and collaborations with diverse partners, building on others' ideas and expressing their own clearly and persuasively.

Source: Adapted from NGA & CCSSO, 2010, pp. 10, 12, 18, 22.

CHAPTER 8

Compare and Contrast

Most informational text follows one of three structures—(1) descriptive, (2) sequential and causal, or (3) comparative. Main Idea Tree lessons help readers organize ideas when the text describes one idea or topic (chapter 6, page 53). Timelines and step maps help students organize ideas with sequence or causation (chapter 7, page 63). A third common type of informational text in elementary grades compares and contrasts two or more elements. Venn diagrams (or double bubbles) and data charts help students organize information when the text is comparing and contrasting members of a category. This chapter describes a lesson framework for teaching students to compare and contrast ideas in one text or multiple texts. Students record information in double bubbles or data charts and write compare-and-contrast summaries based on the information in their diagrams. The lesson consists of two parts; first, the teacher sets the purpose and introduces her class to creating double bubbles and comparing and contrasting using a real-life example. Second, she moves on to a reading lesson that follows the gradual release of responsibility model of instruction. Using the gradual release of responsibility model of instruction, Compare and Contrast combines student partners and teacher-led collaborative conversations to discuss various aspects of the text's content.

A Sample Compare and Contrast Lesson: Part One

To teach her students how to construct double bubbles to compare and contrast ideas, Mrs. H. decides to begin with a real-life topic that most of her students know a lot about—dogs and cats.

Purpose Setting

She says, "Boys and girls, today we are going to talk about pets—and specifically dogs and cats as pets. Raise your hand if you have a pet. Good, now raise your right

TIP

Students in all grades can learn to organize information in double bubbles and data charts.

hand if your pet is a dog and your left hand if your pet is a cat. If you have both pets, raise both hands."

"We have lots of pets in this room," she says, "but some of you don't have pets. I want everyone to put his or her hand down, and this time, raise your right hand if someone you know well—a relative or friend or neighbor—has a dog and your left hand if someone you know well has a cat."

Mrs. H. looks around and says, "Good, I see all your hands, so I know you all know a lot about dogs and cats as pets even if you don't have one. Turn to your partner and talk about the dogs and cats you have or know about. Tell them things like the pet's name, what the dog or cat looks like, what you have to do to take care of these pets, and other important things you know about dogs and cats as pets."

TIP

A turn-and-talk prompt helps students brainstorm while remaining focused.

Mrs. H. has her students seated in talking partners. She often uses the turn-and-talk prompt to get lots of ideas flowing and engage her students in productive talk.

As all the partners talk eagerly to one another, Mrs. H. draws a double bubble on the board and labels it. (See figure 8.1.)

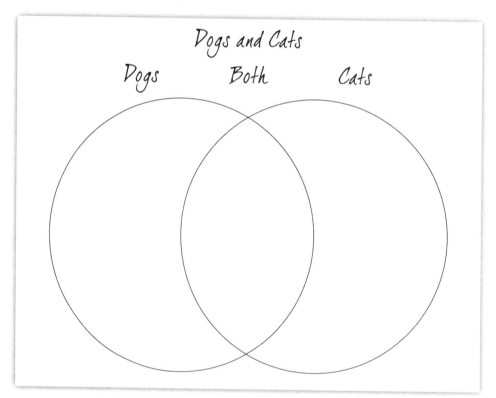

Figure 8.1: Sample double bubble.

"I can tell that you have a lot of ideas about dogs and cats as pets," Mrs. H. says. "We are going to organize our ideas using these two big intersecting circles I call a *double bubble.* On the left side, we are going to write ideas that only apply to dogs, and on the right side, we are going to write ideas that only apply to cats. What are we going to write in this middle part?"

The students instantly understand that characteristics that apply to both dogs and cats will go in the middle.

She continues, "Good, now we are going to start by putting some things in the middle. Remember that these will be features that both cats and dogs share."

The students suggest that they are both mammals and good pets and have four legs, two eyes, two ears, and one tail. Mrs. H. writes this information in the middle. When the students have run out of similarities, Mrs. H. leads them to brainstorm some differences and writes them on the appropriate side. When students think of more similarities, she adds them to the middle. The students eagerly share ideas and complete the double bubble. (See figure 8.2.)

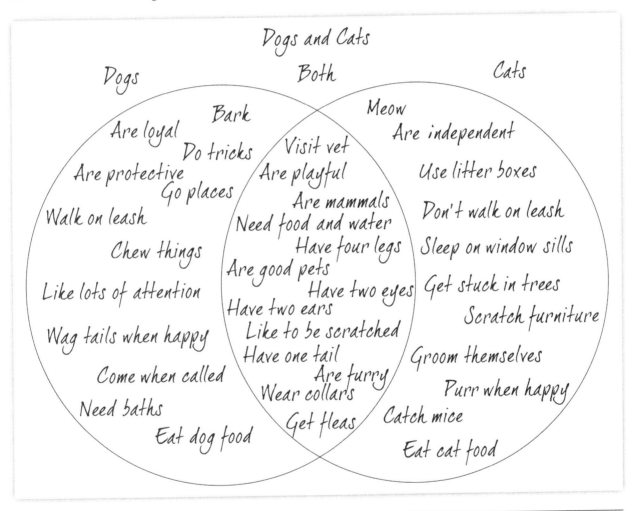

Figure 8.2: Sample double bubble comparing and contrasting dogs and cats.

On the following day, Mrs. H. teaches her students how to write a summary comparing and contrasting the information about dogs and cats. As they review the information in their double bubble, Mrs. H. introduces the words *similarities*, *differences*, *compare*, and *contrast*.

She says, "Let's look at our double bubble. What characteristics of dogs and cats did we put in the middle? Right. We labeled this *both*, and we put things that are the same about both. We call things that are the same *similarities* [she writes *similarities* above *both*], and we say we are comparing cats and dogs [writes *compare* above *both* and *similarities*]. When we are deciding things that are the same or alike about two things, we compare those two things and think of similarities. If we have the similarities in the middle, what do we have on either side?"

Mrs. H. leads the students to see that the things on either side are the differences between cats and dogs and writes the word *differences* above *cats* and *dogs*. Next, she explains that when we list things that are the same, we compare them, but when we list differences, we contrast them. She writes *contrast* above *differences* on each side of the diagram.

"Now we are going to write a summary of what we know about cats and dogs," Mrs. H. says. "I want each of you to start your summary by writing the sentence I am writing on the board on your paper. This sentence will begin the paragraph that compares cats and dogs, so please indent your sentence as I am indenting mine."

She writes the following sentence on the board.

> *Cats and dogs are alike in many ways.*

She says, "This first sentence lets your reader know that you are going to compare cats and dogs and tell about some of their similarities. Now, I am going to add a second sentence that tells some ways they are similar."

> *Cats and dogs are alike in many ways. Cats and dogs both have four legs, two ears, two eyes, and a tail.*

"Now, you add three or four sentences that tell about some of the similarities. You can include my sentence or change it or just add your own ideas," Mrs. H. says.

Students finish their paragraph comparing cats and dogs by writing three or four sentences with similarities. Mrs. H. circulates, monitoring, coaching, and encouraging.

She says, "Good. Now we are going to write a paragraph that compares cats and dogs. Start your second paragraph like this. It's a new paragraph, so don't forget to indent."

> *There are many differences between cats and dogs.*

She continues, "Now, we are going to add sentences that tell about some of the differences. Again, I will write one sentence, and you will add three or four sentences comparing cats and dogs. We have way too many differences for you to include all of them, so decide which differences you think are most important."

> *There are many differences between cats and dogs. Cats groom themselves, but you have to give your dog a bath.*

The students eagerly write a second paragraph, picking and choosing the differences that matter to them.

"Now we need a short paragraph to complete our summary," Mrs. H. says. "So far we have included facts, but I am going to end my summary with my opinion. I am going to tell you which animal I think makes the best pet and give you my reasons for thinking that. Remember, we have learned persuasive writing in which we give reasons for our opinion to try to convince people we are right. As you watch me write my opinion and reasons, think about your own opinion and reasons."

> I think cats make the best pets because they can mostly take care of themselves. You don't have to walk them or give them baths. You can leave them on their own for a few days as long as they have food, water, and a litter box. Cats are independent creatures!

Mrs. H.'s students are always eager to express their opinions, and they quickly write their concluding paragraph. Mrs. H. circulates among students and provides help and encouragement.

The Class Debriefs

When they have finished writing, she lets a few students who chose cats and a few who chose dogs share their paragraphs. Mrs. H.'s class is also quite competitive, and someone asks, "Who won?"

Mrs. H. asks everyone who chose cats and then dogs to raise their hands and gets a quick count. It is close, but dogs get one more vote than cats. Mrs. H. is about to declare dogs the winner when someone points out that Mrs. H.—who chose cats—hasn't voted! The class decides it is a tie, and everyone is happy with this result.

A Sample Compare and Contrast Lesson: Part Two

Once her class understands how to organize compare-and-contrast information in a double bubble, Mrs. H. helps her students transfer this skill to comparing and contrasting information while reading an informational text.

Purpose Setting

Mrs. H. begins the lesson by referring to the double bubble students constructed when they compared and contrasted cats and dogs as pets.

She says, "Sometimes when you read, you need to focus on similarities and differences between the things you are reading about. Today, we are going to construct a double bubble showing the similarities and differences between two countries, China and Japan."

I Do, and You Watch

Mrs. H. begins the lesson by having students get into trios and handing them each one copy of the article.

TIP

Some teachers believe that their class just "can't work in groups." These teachers have often put five or six children in a group, and the groups were not very productive, or two or three students did all the work. Try trios—with a few duets or quartets if your class does not divide equally by three—and you may discover your students can indeed work in groups.

"Here are two articles from your student magazines on China and Japan," she says. "In a few minutes, you are going to read these articles in your trios and organize the information you read in a giant double bubble."

She puts a large piece of paper on the board and draws two intersecting circles, labeling the various portions *China*, *Both*, and *Japan*.

She says, "When reading informational text, study all the visuals first to see what you can learn from them. I am going to see if I can figure out some similarities and differences by looking at the visuals. I see a map of China at the beginning of the China article and a map of Japan at the beginning of the Japan article. I notice that both countries are in Asia, so I am going to write Asia in the middle of our double bubble to show that both China and Japan are on the continent of Asia.

"I also see that both countries have a star next to one city, and I know that a star on a map tells us the capital city. The star on the Japan map is next to Tokyo, and the star on the China map is next to Beijing. I can put that information on the Japan and China parts of my circles."

I Do, and You Help

Addressing the class, she says, "Now, everyone look at the other visuals, and see if you can find things that are the same or different between China and Japan."

One student notices the mountains symbols on both maps and concludes that both countries have mountains. Mrs. H. adds this to the *Both* part of the circles. Another student notices that there is a picture of Chinese children playing basketball and a picture of Japanese children playing baseball. Mrs. H. adds this information to the Japan and China parts of the double bubble.

You Do It Together, and I Help

By now, the students all understand what they are going to do, so Mrs. H. hands each trio a large sheet of paper and a marker. She gives this sheet to the most fluent writer in each group and appoints that student to be the recorder.

She asks the recorder to draw and label the double bubble using the whole sheet of paper, so the students have lots of room to record information. She also instructs the recorder to copy the information from the class double bubble to get them started.

"Once you record the information from our class double bubble," Mrs. H. says, "your trio should study the visuals and add any information you can get from them. Then, read the text and stop whenever you have a similarity or difference to record."

As the trios work together, Mrs. H. circulates, encouraging the trios to talk about what they are reading and decide where to put information.

As each trio finishes, they sign their China and Japan double bubbles and tape them up around the room. The students go around and read what other trios have posted and realize that they have all found many of the same similarities and differences. (See figure 8.3 for a completed double bubble on China and Japan.)

On the following day, Mrs. H. helps students write summaries comparing and contrasting China and Japan. Students take out their writing journals and reread their dog

TIP

Be on the lookout for students who don't help during this phase of the lesson. Some students are just quicker to raise their hands. If a few students are doing all the thinking, have your class think for thirty seconds before letting anyone give an answer. Think time increases both the quantity and quality of student responses.

TIP

Create trios that contain a variety of abilities. Designate the struggling reader to sit in the middle and hold the book. Have the most fluent writer be the recorder.

TIP

In addition to helping and encouraging, conduct formative assessments of your students' ability to compare and contrast by listening in on their discussions.

and cat summaries. She helps them notice that their first paragraph summarized some similarities, and their second paragraph summarized some differences. In their final paragraph, they shared their opinion and gave reasons for that opinion.

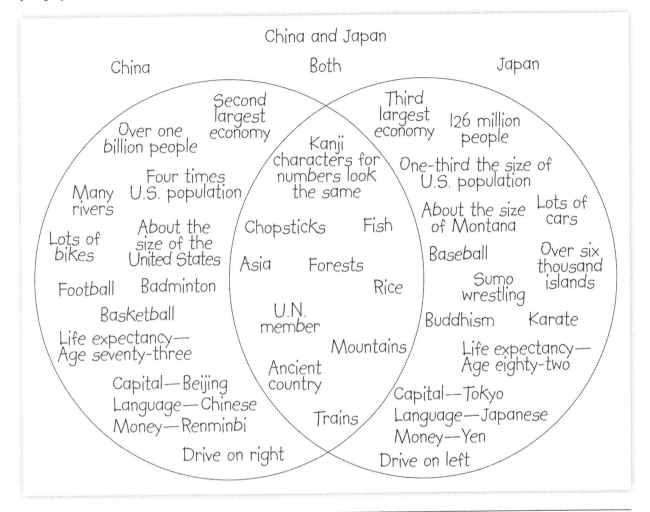

Figure 8.3: Sample completed double bubble for China and Japan.

"That is exactly the structure we are going to use to write our summaries comparing China and Japan," she explains as she writes the starter sentence on the board.

> There are many similarities between China and Japan.

She invites students to suggest a second sentence based on the information in the intersection of the circles. She gets several suggestions and then adds a second sentence to her paragraph.

> There are many similarities between China and Japan. They are both on the continent of Asia, and they both have forests and mountains.

"Copy the introductory sentence, and then add three sentences of your own stating similarities," she says. "You can use the second sentence in my paragraph and then write two more of your own, or you can write all three of your own."

As students write, she circulates among them, coaching, encouraging, and making formative assessments of how well they construct this paragraph. As most students are finishing their paragraphs, she goes to the board and writes a starter sentence for the second paragraph.

> *There are also many differences between China and Japan.*

She continues, "Now we are going to write a paragraph that contrasts China and Japan. Start your second paragraph like this. It's a new paragraph, so don't forget to indent. Who can give me some ideas for my second sentence?"

Mrs. H. listens to their suggestions and adds a second sentence. Again she reminds them that they can use her second sentence and add two more of their own or construct three sentences of their own.

> *There are also many differences between China and Japan. China is much bigger than Japan and has almost ten times as many people.*

The students eagerly write second paragraphs, picking and choosing the differences that matter to them.

"Now we need a short paragraph to complete our summary," Mrs. H. says. "So far we have included facts, but I am going to end my summary with my opinion. I am going to tell you which country I would most like to visit and give you my reasons for this choice. Remember, we have learned persuasive writing in which we give reasons for our opinion to try to convince people we are right. As you watch me write my opinion and reasons, think about your own opinion and reasons."

> *I would like to visit both China and Japan, but if I could only visit one, I would go to Japan. I like baseball and would love to go to a baseball game in Japan. I also like water and would love to visit a country made up of over six thousand islands. Japan is much smaller than China, and I think I could travel through lots of Japan in a week, but I could only see a small part of China.*

The students watch as she writes and then quickly settle in to share their opinions.

The Class Debriefs

When the students have finished writing their opinion paragraphs, they want to tally up their choices. They remind Mrs. H. to vote too. In spite of her Japan vote, China wins by two votes.

TIP

You can also use double bubbles to compare characters, themes, plots, or settings from narratives including poems, plays, and stories.

In a later lesson on the planets, Mrs. H. uses the same process for double bubbles to transition students into organizing and comparing three or more items of a category on a data chart. (See figure 8.4.) Mrs. H. and the class complete this part of the chart using the "I do, and you watch" and "I do, and you help" phases of the gradual release of responsibility model of instruction. The class works in trios to complete the chart.

Planet	Size (1 = Biggest)	Distance From Sun	Earth Days in Year	Other Characteristics
Earth	5	93 million miles (Third)	365	Plants, animals, people, gravity
Jupiter	1	484 million miles (Fifth)	One Jupiter year equals twelve Earth years	Mostly gases Sixty-two moons Very hot
Mars				
Mercury				
Saturn				
Venus				
Uranus				
Neptune				

Figure 8.4: Sample data chart for the planets in our solar system.

Planning and Teaching a Compare and Contrast Lesson

There is not a lot of planning needed to teach a compare and contrast lesson. When using double bubbles, make sure the texts students are reading compare and contrast two things. Draw and label the bubbles so students know that they are reading to compare and contrast by looking for similarities and differences. When students are comfortable with double bubbles, teach them how to use data charts to compare and contrast multiple members of a category. Use the following eight steps to teach a Compare and Contrast lesson.

1. Clarify what *compare* and *contrast* mean. Use a real-life example to introduce double bubbles and compare and contrast something students know a lot about.

2. Once students understand how to organize information comparing and contrasting two things in the real world, help them transfer this ability to text. Set the purpose for the lesson by telling students that when they are reading they often need to compare and contrast two things, looking for

similarities and differences. Creating a double bubble will help them organize the information they are learning.

3. Organize trios with students of different reading and writing abilities. Give trios one copy of the text you have chosen and a large sheet of paper. Have the recorder draw and label two large intersecting circles.

4. Model for students how you compare and contrast and where you write the similarities and differences by recording one similarity and one difference on your double bubble ("I do, and you watch").

5. Let students help you add a few more similarities and differences to the class double bubble ("I do, and you help").

6. Have students read the text, stopping to add similarities and differences to their double bubble. If the text is informational, encourage them to find out all they can from the visuals before they read the text. Circulate, coach, and formatively assess how the groups are interacting and how well they are able to compare and contrast various features of text ("You do it together, and I help").

7. Teach students to write compare-and-contrast summaries in which they write one paragraph summarizing similarities and another summarizing differences. Have them add a concluding paragraph if appropriate.

8. When students are comfortable comparing and contrasting two things, introduce data charts to help them compare and contrast three or more items, ideas, or characters. Use the same procedures you used for double bubbles to teach data charts.

Compare and Contrast Lessons Across the Year

You will find many opportunities to help your students compare and contrast information in all areas of your curriculum throughout the school year. As students demonstrate their ability to compare and contrast, gradually fade out the modeling and helping steps, and let the trios construct double bubbles or data charts for the entire text. Similarly, as students learn how to construct compare-and-contrast paragraphs, fade out the modeling and helping steps in writing the paragraphs. When your formative assessments indicate that most of your students can compare and contrast, have them construct a double bubble or data chart and write a summary paragraph independently ("You do, and I watch").

To help students apply their compare-and-contrast skills when reading on their own, observe what your students are reading during their independent reading time. For students who are reading a text that compares and contrasts two or more elements, suggest that they construct a double bubble or data chart to organize the facts. Let students who decide to construct one share it with the class.

How Compare and Contrast Lessons Teach the Standards

Reading anchor standard nine and Reading literature standard three (CCRA.R.9 and RL.3) focus on comparing and contrasting—characters, stories, authors, and important information. Compare and Contrast lessons teach students to pay attention to these similarities and differences. When students write summaries comparing and contrasting information, they work on Writing anchor standard two (CCRA.W.2). The lesson teaches Writing anchor standard ten (CCRA.W.10), because the pieces students produce make a contribution to the routine writing the Common Core expects all students to do. The compare-and-contrast discussions students have in their trios and with the whole class teach Speaking and Listening anchor standard one (CCRA.SL.1).

CCSS in a Text Features Scavenger Hunt Lesson

Text Features Scavenger Hunt is a lesson framework that teaches students how to use the special text features and visuals that are integral to informational text. When you lead students through this lesson several times and gradually release responsibility to them, you are helping them learn the reading, speaking and listening, and language skills in the following standards.

Reading

RI.2.4: Determine the meaning of words and phrases in a text relevant to a *grade 2 topic or subject area*.

RI.3–5.4: Determine the meaning of general academic and domain-specific words and phrases in a text relevant to a *grade-level topic or subject area*.

RI.1–2.5: Know and use various text features to locate key facts or information in a text.

RI.3.5: Use text features and search tools (such as key words, sidebars, and hyperlinks) to locate information relevant to a given topic efficiently.

RI.2.7: Explain how specific images (such as a diagram showing how a machine works) contribute to and clarify a text.

RI.3.7: Use information gained from illustrations (such as maps and photographs) and the words in a text to demonstrate understanding of the text (such as *where*, *when*, *why*, and *how* key events occur).

RI.4.7: Interpret information presented visually, orally, or quantitatively (such as in charts, graphs, diagrams, timelines, animations, or interactive elements on webpages), and explain how the information contributes to an understanding of the text in which it appears.

Speaking and Listening

CCRA.SL.1: Prepare for and participate effectively in a range of conversations and collaborations with diverse partners, building on others' ideas and expressing their own clearly and persuasively.

Language

CCRA.L.4: Determine or clarify the meaning of unknown and multiple-meaning words and phrases by using context clues, analyzing meaningful word parts, and consulting general and specialized reference materials, as appropriate.

Source: Adapted from NGA & CCSSO, 2010, pp. 13–14, 22, 25.

CHAPTER 9

Text Features Scavenger Hunt

Look at any piece of informational text—a magazine article, a textbook chapter, an informational book—and you will see many features you don't see in stories, poems, or plays. The most noticeable feature of informational text is a variety of visuals; drawings, photos, maps, charts, graphs, and diagrams are common features of informational text. Additionally, informational texts contain headings that signal the main ideas of each section and, sometimes, subheadings. Within the text, you will occasionally notice bold words. These are important vocabulary terms that are often defined in the text and sometimes further clarified in a glossary. Most informational texts contain words students may not know how to pronounce; some texts even provide pronunciations in parentheses next to vocabulary words. If the text is divided into chapters, you can probably find a table of contents in the beginning and an index at the end, which will help you quickly locate specific information within the text.

With all these helpful features, students should be more successful at reading informational text than they are at reading stories. Often the opposite is true, however. In our experience, many elementary students comprehend stories better than they comprehend informational text. How can that be? Most likely, the explanation is simple. Most students don't know what all these helpful features are for or how to use them. Text Features Scavenger Hunt teaches students to maximize use of all the special features they find in informational text. In order to complete the hunt, they have to use all the features a particular piece of informational text contains. Focusing attention on bold words and having students either consult the glossary or figure out the meaning from the text help students meet Reading informational text and Language anchor standards four (RI.4 and CCRA.L.4). Using the gradual release of responsibility model of instruction, Text Features Scavenger Hunt combines student trios and teacher-led collaborative conversations to discuss various aspects of the text's content.

TIP

You can do Text Features Scavenger Hunt with most first graders in the spring, if you limit the features you focus on to two or three and include no more than ten questions.

A Sample Text Features Scavenger Hunt Lesson

Following is a sample Text Features Scavenger Hunt lesson in a social studies class. The students are about to read a chapter about the Great Depression. First, they will go on a scavenger hunt, learning from the visuals and other special features of the text. This is their first scavenger hunt, so Mr. Y. begins by having teams scavenge for items in the classroom. Then, the students scavenge for features in the text.

Purpose Setting and Vocabulary Building

Mr. Y. begins the lesson by asking if any of the students has gone on a scavenger hunt. Only two students have done this. They share their experiences and explain that you have to find specific items within a limited amount of time. The team who finds the most wins the scavenger hunt.

Next, Mr. Y. asks if anyone can guess why we call it a *scavenger hunt*. One student volunteers that some animals are scavengers. Using examples students relate to—raccoons rummaging in trash cans and vultures eating roadkill—Mr. Y. leads the students to realize that a scavenger is someone who finds things and eats or collects them.

He says, "Soon we are going to scavenge for information in a chapter we will read later this week. But we are going to begin by doing a quick scavenger hunt in our classroom. Please gather in your reading trios, and I will give you a list of things I want you to find in the classroom. You will have three minutes to find as many of the items on the list as you can and write what you found on the classroom scavenger hunt sheet. The team who finds the most items will win the scavenger hunt."

The students assemble themselves into trios.

Mr. Y. hands each trio a classroom scavenger hunt sheet (see figure 9.1) and sets the timer for three minutes.

When the timer sounds, Mr. Y. tells students to finish writing the item they are on, and then together the class tallies up the score. The winning team found seventeen items in three minutes. As the students cheer, they want to know if they get a prize.

"Bragging rights," responds Mr. Y.

Next, Mr. Y. shows students several pages of a chapter book they have recently read and several pages from the social studies book.

He says, "I know you haven't had time to read these pages, but which one do you think is a story, and which one is informational?"

The class quickly decides that the one with no pictures is the story and the one with "all the pictures" is information. Mr. Y. then flips through the pages of the social studies text and asks what, besides the pictures, is different about the informational text. He leads his students to notice that the social studies text contains maps, charts, bold words, and headings.

He says, "We call these special things that informational texts have but story texts don't usually have *informational text features*. Today, we are going to look at this chapter in our social studies book and see how much we can learn from these special text features. We are going to go on a scavenger hunt in our book and see how much information we can find just by focusing on pictures, captions, graphs, charts, bold words, and other special features of informational text."

TIP

Seize every opportunity to build meanings for words, and you will increase the size of all your students' vocabularies!

TIP

In our experience working with teachers, three is the magic number for small-group work in most elementary classrooms. If the group size is too large, some students spend time vying for control of the group, and other students just sit and let the bossy ones do the work!

TIP

Hand the book to the least able reader in the trio. There is status in holding the book!

Classroom Scavenger Hunt

Directions: You have three minutes to find and write the name of an object that matches the description.

Something green _____	Something opaque _____	Something made of cloth _____
Something rectangular _____	Something oval _____	Something taller than Mr. Y. _____
Something you can see through _____	Something that can move _____	Something white _____
Something made of glass _____	Something growing _____	Something breakable _____
Something alive _____	Something brown _____	Something you can put things in _____
Something made of wood _____	Something liquid _____	Something you can't move _____
Something red _____	Something you can read _____	Something you can eat _____
Something you can write on _____	Something smaller than your thumb _____	Something that can talk _____
Something made of plastic _____	Something rough _____	Something you can turn off _____
Something eight inches long _____	Something shiny _____	Something you can't reach _____

Figure 9.1: Sample classroom scavenger hunt sheet.

I Do, and You Watch

Mr. Y. hands out one copy of the social studies book to each trio and asks the students to turn to page 369.

He says, "Now we are going to go on a scavenger hunt in our social studies books. We are going to use the visuals and other features of the book to find answers to questions. Just as in our classroom scavenger hunt, you will have a limited amount of time—twenty minutes—and probably won't be able to find everything, but that's

TIP

Hand the sheet to the most able writer. The writing will go much more quickly!

OK. At the end of twenty minutes, we will come together and see what you found and determine the winner. I am going to do a few for you to get you started, and then the twenty minutes will start."

Mr. Y. hands the Text Features Scavenger Hunt sheet (see figure 9.2) to one student in each trio.

Text Features Scavenger Hunt

Directions: Use the visuals and other special text features from your book to answer these questions. Indicate where you found the answers. You have twenty minutes to find as many answers as you can. Your team will get one point for every correct answer and another point for writing where you found the answer.

Question	Your Answer	Where Did You Find This Answer?
What instrument did Louis Armstrong play?		
What was the name of the dog on RCA's label?		
What is the name of a Charlie Chaplin movie?		
How many Ford cars were sold in 1920? In 1929? (Two points)		
What new buildings were built in New York City in the 1920s?		
What year had the most business failures?		
About how many people lost their jobs in 1933?		
What five states were in the dust bowl region? (Five points)		
Which president began the New Deal program?		
In what year did Charles Lindbergh fly across the Atlantic?		
What is the fifth step in assembling a car in Henry Ford's factory?		
What is the first major heading in chapter 5?		
What is the last major heading in chapter 5?		

Question	Your Answer	Where Did You Find This Answer?
Use the index to decide on what page you will find information about:		
• Herbert Hoover		
• Clarence Birdseye		
• Henry Ford		
Find three bold words and write their glossary definitions.		
•		
•		
•		
Following are pronunciations for three words. Write the word and the page on which you found it.		
ur-buh-nuh-ZAY-shun		
in-dus-tree-uh-luh-ZAY-shun		
byu-RAH-kruh-see		

Figure 9.2: Sample Text Features Scavenger Hunt sheet.

Mr. Y. reads the first question aloud and then says, "I see a picture of Louis Armstrong at the top of page 369, and he has a trumpet. I will write *trumpet* in this box and *photo on page 369* in the next box." (See figure 9.3.)

What instrument did Louis Armstrong play?	*trumpet*	*photo on page 369*

Figure 9.3: Sample Text Features Scavenger Hunt sheet answer.

Looking again at page 369, he says, "You don't have to go in order on a scavenger hunt; I see the answer to another question on this page, so I will fill that one in." (See figure 9.4, page 90.)

What is the first major heading in chapter 5?	*New Forms of Expression*	*heading on page 369*

Figure 9.4: Sample Text Features Scavenger Hunt sheet answer.

"The writer in each trio should fill in these two answers on your sheet," he says.

I Do, and You Help

"Now, help me do two more," Mr. Y. says, "and then I will turn you loose to find the rest of the answers. Who can find the answer to the second question?"

Someone quickly locates the photo of the dog and reads the caption that accompanies the photo. Mr. Y. and the writer in each trio fill in their answers. (See figure 9.5.)

What was the name of the dog on RCA's label?	*Nipper*	*caption on page 370*

Figure 9.5: Sample Text Features Scavenger Hunt sheet answer.

Mr. Y. says, "Good, now go to the very bottom of the classroom scavenger hunt sheet. The word is written the way it is pronounced: byu-RAH-kruh-see. We need to find that word and figure out what it is. Help me find it."

A student quickly finds the word and page, and everyone records this answer. (See figure 9.6.)

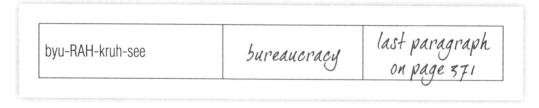

byu-RAH-kruh-see	*bureaucracy*	*last paragraph on page 371*

Figure 9.6: Sample Text Features Scavenger Hunt sheet answer.

You Do It Together, and I Help

Mr. Y. reiterates the directions on the classroom scavenger hunt sheet: "Use the visuals and other special text features from your book to answer the remaining questions. Indicate where you found the answers. You have twenty minutes to find as many answers as you can. Your team will get one point for every correct answer and another point for writing where you found the answer. Your time begins now!" Mr. Y. starts the timer.

The students quickly and eagerly get busy finding answers and writing them down. Mr. Y. circulates and reminds one trio that the students also need to include the page number where they found the information. For twenty minutes, the classroom is filled with "good noise" as students work to beat the clock.

The Class Debriefs

The timer sounds, and Mr. Y. lets students finish the answers they are writing and then demands that everyone put his or her pencil down. Together, Mr. Y. and the class check the answer to each question, looking at the visual or special feature that provided the answer and explaining how they figured out the answers. Each team totals its points, and after Mr. Y. double-checks the scores, there is a three-way tie. Three teams cheer and enjoy their bragging rights. (See figure 9.7 for a completed Text Features Scavenger Hunt sheet.)

Text Features Scavenger Hunt

Directions: Use the visuals and other special text features from your book to answer these questions. Indicate where you found the answers. You have twenty minutes to find as many answers as you can. Your team will get one point for every correct answer and another point for writing where you found the answer.

Question	Your Answer	Where Did You Find This Answer?
What instrument did Louis Armstrong play?	trumpet	photo on page 369
What was the name of the dog on RCA's label?	Nipper	caption on page 370
What is the name of a Charlie Chaplin movie?	The Kid	poster on page 371
How many Ford cars were sold in 1920? In 1929? (Two points)	2 million in 1920 and 4.5 million in 1929	picture graph on page 375
What new buildings were built in New York City in the 1920s?	skyscrapers	picture graph on page 370
What year had the most business failures?	1931	photo caption on page 372
About how many people lost their jobs in 1933?	13,000	bar graph on page 371
What five states were in the dust bowl region? (Five points)	Colorado, Texas, Kansas, Oklahoma, and New Mexico	map on page 370

Figure 9.7: Sample completed Text Features Scavenger Hunt sheet.
Continued →

Question	Your Answer	Where Did You Find This Answer?
Which president began the New Deal program?	Franklin D. Roosevelt	photo caption on page 373
In what year did Charles Lindbergh fly across the Atlantic?	1927	timeline on page 372
What is the fifth step in assembling a car in Henry Ford's factory?	Wheels and radiators are attached.	diagram on page 375
What is the first major heading in chapter 5?	New Forms of Expression	heading on page 369
What is the last major heading in chapter 5?	New Deal	heading on page 376
Find three bold words and write their glossary definitions.		
• stock market	a place where people can buy and sell shares in a business	paragraph two on page 373
• Depression	a time of little economic growth when there are few jobs and people have little money	paragraph four on page 366
• consumer goods	products made for personal use	paragraph one on page 365
Following are pronunciations for three words. Write the word and the page on which you found it.		
ur-buh-nuh-ZAY-shun	urbanization	on page 372
in-dus-tree-uh-luh-ZAY-shun	industrialization	on page 373
byu-RAH-kruh-see	bureaucracy	last paragraph on page 371

Mr. Y. asks each student to construct one new question that visuals or special features can help answer. Mr. Y. picks a few of these and reads them to the class, and everyone hunts for the answers.

Planning and Teaching a Text Features Scavenger Hunt Lesson

To plan the lesson, choose a piece of informational text you want students to read, and create questions that will direct their attention to all the special text features in that text. Decide how long you will allow students to hunt—giving them a little less time than you think they need will create a sense of urgency. If your students do not know what a scavenger hunt is or have never been on one, engage them in a real scavenger hunt in your classroom or school before starting the Text Features Scavenger Hunt lesson. Use the following six steps when teaching a Text Features Scavenger Hunt lesson.

1. Tell students the purpose of the lesson. If this is the first Text Features Scavenger Hunt they have gone on, show them some story text and informational text and help them notice the special features of informational text. Note that you can learn a lot of information just by focusing on special text features.

2. Put your students in trios. Give each group one copy of the text to use for the hunt and one Text Features Scavenger Hunt sheet. Hand the sheet to your most fluent writer and the book to the least fluent reader in each group. This setup allows the writer to jot answers quickly and conveys status for the reader.

3. For the first several scavenger hunts, use the "I do, and you watch" and "I do, and you help" gradual release of responsibility phases to model the Text Features Scavenger Hunt. This will get them off to a successful start with the activity.

4. Set a timer for twenty minutes, and have students work together to find the answers and record the answers and where they found them. Circulate and provide help to teams as needed.

5. When the time is up, go over the answers and their text locations. Talk about each special text feature and how it helps answer questions. Have teams tally their points. Check the tallies of the winning teams, and reward them with bragging rights.

6. Have students individually construct one more scavenger hunt question. Choose a few questions and have classmates solve them as time permits.

Text Features Scavenger Hunt Lessons Across the Year

When your observations of the teams indicate that everyone understands how to use the various text features, fade out the "I do, and you watch" and "I do, and you help" phases. When almost all students understand how to use the various text features, have students complete a Text Features Scavenger Hunt independently. Use these assessments to determine students who need more instruction on certain text features.

How Text Features Scavenger Hunt Lessons Teach the Standards

Text Features Scavenger Hunt lessons teach students to use special features of informational text. This lesson framework teaches Reading informational text standard five

(RI.5), which requires students to learn to use headings, glossaries, indexes, and more to locate information. Reading informational text standard seven (RI.7) focuses on the visuals—maps, charts, graphs, and others. Because these lessons focus on vocabulary in informational text, students are increasing the size of their meaning vocabularies, as Reading informational text standard four (RI.4) and Language anchor standard four (CCRA.L.4) require. The discussions students have while on the scavenger hunt help teach Speaking and Listening anchor standard one (CCRA.SL.1).

CCSS in a Preview-Predict-Confirm Lesson

Preview-Predict-Confirm is a lesson framework to use with any informational text that has a lot of visuals, including photos, maps, charts, and diagrams. When you lead students through this lesson several times and gradually release responsibility to them, you are helping them learn the reading, writing, speaking and listening, and language skills in the following standards.

Reading
RI.2.4: Determine the meaning of words and phrases in a text relevant to a *grade 2 topic or subject area*.

RI.2.7: Explain how specific images (such as a diagram showing how a machine works) contribute to and clarify a text.

RI.3–5.4: Determine the meaning of general academic and domain-specific words and phrases in a text relevant to a *grade-level topic or subject area*.

RI.3.7: Use information gained from illustrations (such as maps and photographs) and the words in a text to demonstrate understanding of the text (such as where, when, why, and how key events occur).

RI.4.7: Interpret information presented visually, orally, or quantitatively (such as in charts, graphs, diagrams, timelines, animations, or interactive elements on webpages) and explain how the information contributes to an understanding of the text in which it appears.

RI.5.7: Draw on information from multiple print or digital sources, demonstrating the ability to locate an answer to a question quickly or to solve a problem efficiently.

Writing
CCRA.W.2: Write informative/explanatory texts to examine and convey complex ideas and information clearly and accurately through the effective selection, organization, and analysis of content.

CCRA.W.10: Write routinely over extended time frames (time for research, reflection, and revision) and shorter time frames (a single sitting or a day or two) for a range of tasks, purposes, and audiences.

Speaking and Listening
CCRA.SL.1: Prepare for and participate effectively in a range of conversations and collaborations with diverse partners, building on others' ideas and expressing their own clearly and persuasively.

Language
CCRA.L.4: Determine or clarify the meaning of unknown and multiple-meaning words and phrases by using context clues, analyzing meaningful word parts, and consulting general and specialized reference materials, as appropriate.

Source: Adapted from NGA & CCSSO, 2010, pp. 13–14, 18, 22, 25.

CHAPTER 10

Preview-Predict-Confirm

Preview-Predict-Confirm is a lesson framework that teaches students to use the visuals in an informational text to build vocabulary and make predictions (Yopp & Yopp, 2004). Using the visuals to anticipate and understand text is the major focus. The lesson begins with students seated in their trios and talking about ten to fifteen visuals from a text they will read. Students have twenty seconds to look at each visual, talk about it, and try to predict words they will read connected to the visual. Next, students have eight minutes to write as many words as they can that they think will occur. At the end of eight minutes, students look at their words and choose one word they think all the other groups will also have, one word they think is unique to their group, and one word they are most interested in. Next, the trios read the text together. They put a check on each word they listed that actually occurred and add five words they wish they had thought of. The class reconvenes and shares their discoveries. At the end of the lesson, students write a short paragraph using as many of their words as they can to tell what they learned. Using the gradual release of responsibility model of instruction, Preview-Predict-Confirm combines student trios and teacher-led conversations to focus on academic vocabulary.

A Sample Preview-Predict-Confirm Lesson

Following is a sample lesson using a book about penguins. (Consider using *Penguins!* by Gail Gibbons.)

Purpose Setting

Mrs. B. begins the lesson by showing students a few of the visuals from a book about penguins. Students describe the visuals and name things they see. Mrs. B. also asks them to predict what they think the text on the page will be about based on the visuals.

She tells them, "I can tell that you already know a lot about penguins, and the pictures help remind you of what you know. When we study the visuals before we read, our brains make connections to what we already know, and we can predict what the text might tell us. The visuals also make us think of questions—things we want to know—and when we read, we find out if what we read answers those questions. Today, we are going to work on connecting what we know to visuals and predicting which words the author will use to tell us more about penguins."

I Do, and You Watch

Mrs. B. seats her students in trios. She has arranged the trios to have a strong reader and writer in each group and has divided her English learners among the trios.

"I am going to show you some visuals from the text," she says, "and you will have twenty seconds to talk about each. Try to name everything you see in the visual, and talk about what you think the text on this page—which I have covered—will tell you. I will show you what I want you to do on this first visual."

She shows the first visual for twenty seconds and talks about what she sees and what things she might learn from the text on this page.

She comments aloud to the class, "I see lots of penguins, and it looks like they are climbing up the ice and then sliding down. Are those icebergs they're sliding on? I wonder where those penguins are."

She removes this visual from the screen and then shows the students a prediction sheet with the word *penguins* in the middle box and lots of empty boxes surrounding it (see figure 10.1).

	Penguins	

Figure 10.1: Sample prediction sheet.

She says, "After you have talked about all the visuals, I am going to give your trio a sheet that looks like this [see figure 10.2]. Your trio will have eight minutes to write words in the boxes that you think you will read based on what you saw in the visuals. I am going to begin by putting in the words *climbing*, *sliding*, and *iceberg*, because I think those words will be in the book."

climbing		
sliding		
iceberg		
	Penguins	

Figure 10.2: Sample prediction sheet with possible words based on the visuals.

I Do, and You Help

Mrs. B. says, "Now, I am going to show you the second visual. Talk with your trio for twenty seconds about what you see. Name everything you can, and try to think of questions the text might answer."

She shows the second visual, and the groups talk animatedly for twenty seconds. After twenty seconds, she removes the visual and asks them to help her list words they think they will see, and they suggest she add *diving*, *swimming*, and *ocean*. She writes these words in boxes on the penguin sheet.

You Do It Together, and I Help

She says, "Now I am going to show you the rest of the visuals for twenty seconds each. Talk about each, and try to come up with words that you can add to the sheet, which I will give you when you have seen all the visuals."

Mrs. B. shows them the remaining ten visuals, which include a map, chart, and diagram in addition to pictures. She has covered all the words—except for any labels

TIP

Don't give students the sheet until they have had twenty seconds to talk. If they have the sheet, they will want to start writing words, and this will greatly decrease the amount of talking they do about each visual.

or captions that go with the visuals. The students talk excitedly about each visual. She overhears the following conversations as students view the visuals.

"Those are seals and walruses and whales. I bet whales eat penguins."

"What is that funny-looking little thing? It looks like a bug or maybe a shrimp."

"There's an egg. Those must be the mother and father penguins."

"The mother penguin is feeding the baby. I think she chews the food and then regurgitates it." "What does *regurgitate* mean?" "It's like when you throw up." "Oh, gross!"

"Those penguins are all together. They look like they are in a huddle like at a football game. I think that helps them stay warm."

"That's a map that shows the world and where different penguins live. That map has a lot of words that will for sure be in the book: *Antarctica, Australia, South Pole,* and *Pacific Ocean.* We need more time to look at that map!"

"What's happening? I think it must be an oil spill. Look at that brown stuff in the water. I bet penguins are going to get covered in oil. Someone will need to rescue them."

"That's a penguin caught in that fishing net. How is he going to get out?"

When the students have viewed and talked about all the images, Mrs. B. gives them the penguin prediction sheet. She hands the sheet to the most fluent writer in each group and asks that person to be the recorder. She lets the trios copy the six words predicted based on the first two visuals and then gives them eight minutes to write words they think will occur in the text based on the other visuals. The students talk eagerly and try to fill in all the boxes before the time is up. (See figure 10.3 for one trio's completed sheet.)

TIP

Remind students that the words need to be topic related (words like and, the, *and* of *are not allowed).*

climbing	diving	white
sliding	swimming	cold
iceberg	ocean	waddle
fins	emperor	beak
shrimp	**Penguins**	South Pole
frozen	net	oil
birds	trapped	predators
regurgitate	endangered	eggs
fish	Australia	tuxedos
ice	huddle	Antarctica

Figure 10.3: Sample student-completed prediction sheet.

When the eight minutes are up, she hands each trio three different-colored strips of paper and then explains the next task.

She says, "On the red strip, I want you to decide on a word that you think is so obvious that all the other trios will also have this word. We call this word a *common word* because it is probably common to all the groups. I am going to write a *C* on this red strip to remind you what goes on the red strip.

"On the green strip, I want you to write a word your trio thought of but you don't think any of the other trios thought of. We call this a *unique word* because it might be unique to your group. I am going to write a *U* on this green strip to remind you what goes on the green strip.

"On the blue strip, write the word your trio thinks is the most interesting. I am going to write an *I* on this blue strip to remind you what goes on the blue strip. You have two minutes to talk about your words and decide on your common, unique, and most interesting word."

After two minutes, Mrs. B. gathers the class together and has each trio show the word it has chosen as common, unique, and interesting. (See figure 10.4 for one trio's word strips.)

TIP

It doesn't matter which words they choose. The purpose of this step is to get them talking about the words!

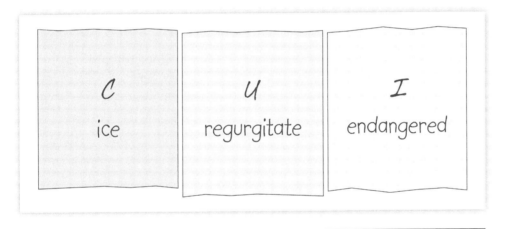

Figure 10.4: Sample common, unique, and interesting words.

She says, "Now I am giving your trio one copy of the book. The person I hand the book to needs to sit in the middle, and you all need to read the pages together and decide which of the words you thought would be in this book are actually there. Put a star on each word that you find in the book."

The students read the book and are delighted to find that many of the words they predicted are actually in the book. As trios finish reading, Mrs. B. asks them to turn their sheets over, go back through the book, and list five words they wish they had thought of.

The Class Debriefs

When the groups have finished reading the book and starring the words, Mrs. B. gathers the class together and asks for volunteers to share some words that occurred in both places and some that didn't. The group that thought of *regurgitate* is disappointed to find that the book didn't use this. Mrs. B. sympathizes with the students and tells

TIP

Students work together and interact more when they have just one copy of the text. Let the struggling reader in the group hold the book and sit in the middle. It shows that student he or she has an important job to do.

them that perhaps the author thought they couldn't understand the word *regurgitate*, but she knows how smart they are. The three trios that finish first list words they wish they had thought of and share their words and reasons why they should have thought of those words.

Mrs. B. ends the lesson by having students summarize some of what they learned about penguins. They use a paragraph frame they have previously learned to summarize informational text.

"I have learned many interesting facts about _____. I learned that _____. I also learned that _____ and _____. But the most interesting fact I learned about _____ is that _____."

Planning and Teaching a Preview-Predict-Confirm Lesson

Select twelve to fifteen visuals from a text, including photos, maps, charts, and diagrams. Scan these into a presentation or cover the words (except for labels included in visuals). Assign your students to trios, making sure to have a strong reader and writer in each. Write the topic word in the center of a thirty-box sheet, and provide three different-colored strips of paper for each trio so students can write their common, unique, and interesting words.

You can adapt the Preview-Predict-Confirm lesson framework to use in kindergarten or first grade by using just five or six visuals, stopping after students have had twenty seconds to talk about each visual, and asking trios to share the words they think will be on that page. As students read the text, or you read it to them, stop on each page, and ask your students which words they predicted actually occurred. Use the following nine steps when teaching a Preview-Predict-Confirm lesson.

1. Tell students the purpose for the lesson. Point out that by studying the visuals before you read informational text, you can make connections to what you already know and predict some words that you might see and some questions the text will answer.

2. Use the "I do, and you watch" and "I do, and you help" phases for the first visuals so that students will understand what they are expected to do.

3. Show the remaining visuals, and give trios twenty seconds to talk about each.

4. Give trios a sheet with thirty boxes and the topic in the middle box. Hand the sheet to the fastest writer in the group, and ask that student to be the recorder. Tell students that they have eight minutes to try to fill up the boxes with words they think will be in the text they are about to read.

5. After eight minutes, give each trio three different-colored strips of paper. Give trios two minutes to choose a common word—a word they think all the other groups will also have; a unique word—a word they don't think any other group will have; and an interesting word—a word they want to learn more about. Have them write the words on the designated color strip with a marker, big enough so that everyone can see it when the class reconvenes.

6. After two minutes, gather the class together. Have groups hold up their paper with the word they think is common, and see how many other trios did indeed include that word on their list. Next, have groups hold up their unique words and determine if each word is truly unique to one group. If students ask what a word means, let the group with that word define it. Finally, have each group display the word the students are most interested in.

7. Give trios one copy of the text, and ask them to read it together. Have them put a star on each word on their sheet that actually occurred. When groups finish before others, have them look back through the text and choose five words they wish they had thought of and write these five words on the back of their sheets.

8. Gather the students and discuss which words actually occurred. If some sophisticated words did not occur in the text, brag on the group that chose the word, and tell the students that their word would have been better! Let groups who had time to list words they wish they had thought of share some of these words and their reasons for choosing them.

9. Have students write a paragraph including some facts they learned. Allow them to look back at the text and their list of words as they write, and encourage them to use text-specific words related to the topic. Use a paragraph frame if they need this kind of support.

Preview-Predict-Confirm Lessons Across the Year

In subsequent lessons as students demonstrate their ability to predict key words based on visuals, gradually fade out the modeling and helping steps, and let the trios talk about and come up with words for all the visuals. When your formative assessments indicate that most of your students can predict words based on the visuals, have them do this independently ("You do, and I watch").

How Preview-Predict-Confirm Lessons Teach the Standards

Reading standard seven for informational text (RI.7) focuses on teaching students to use text visuals to integrate information with words. Preview-Predict-Confirm lessons teach students to interpret visuals and think about the words used to flesh out the information in the visuals. Because these lessons focus on vocabulary in informational text, students increase the size of their meaning vocabularies, as Reading informational text standard four (RI.4) and Language anchor standard four (CCRA.L.4) require. The brief writing students do at the end of the lesson teaches students how to write summaries including key vocabulary, as Writing anchor standard two (CCRA.W.2) requires. The lesson teaches Writing anchor standard ten (CCRA.W.10), because the pieces students produce make a contribution to the routine writing the Common Core expects all students to do. The discussions students have about the visuals help teach Speaking and Listening anchor standard one (CCRA.SL.1).

CCSS in a Point of View Lesson

Point of View lessons help students determine the point of view of narrators, characters, and authors on events or topics and compare and contrast them with their own points of view. When you lead students through this lesson several times and gradually release responsibility to them, you are helping them learn the reading, writing, and speaking and listening skills in the following standards.

Reading

CCRA.R.1: Read closely to determine what the text says explicitly and to make logical inferences from it; cite specific textual evidence when writing or speaking to support conclusions drawn from the text.

CCRA.R.6: Assess how point of view or purpose shapes the content and style of a text.

RI.4.8: Explain how an author uses reasons and evidence to support particular points in a text.

Writing

CCRA.W.1: Write arguments to support claims in an analysis of substantive topics or texts, using valid reasoning and relevant and sufficient evidence.

CCRA.W.10: Write routinely over extended time frames (time for research, reflection, and revision) and shorter time frames (a single sitting or a day or two) for a range of tasks, purposes, and audiences.

Speaking and Listening

CCRA.SL.1: Prepare for and participate effectively in a range of conversations and collaborations with diverse partners, building on others' ideas and expressing their own clearly and persuasively.

Source: Adapted from NGA & CCSSO, 2010, pp. 10, 14, 18, 22.

CHAPTER 11

Point of View

At different grade levels, students are expected to determine who is narrating an event; compare first- and third-person accounts of events; describe how a narrator's, character's, or author's point of view influences events and situations; and compare their own point of view with that of a narrator, character, or author. Point of view has different applications in reading. The most important distinction is between literature and informational text. In most literary texts, there are one or more characters. Literary texts also have a narrator who may simply be the author or who may be a major or minor character in the narrative. Reading anchor standard six (CCRA.R.6) requires students to understand point of view, to identify the narrator of a literary text, and to discern a narrator's or character's point of view and distinguish it from their own. By contrast, informational text has an author who makes one or more points about a topic. Reading literature standard six (RL.6) and Reading informational text standard eight (RI.8) expect students to comprehend the author's general purpose for writing informational text, the author's point of view about the topic, and the reasons and evidence the author presents to support the point or points he or she is making. Finally, students must differentiate the author's point of view from theirs.

At first glance, this all sounds complicated and a bit unwieldy for elementary students (and it is challenging!), but in reality, every one of us—including young students—has a point of view that shapes how we view events and situations and how we feel and think about them. Over time, taught with a variety of both literary and informational texts, Point of View lessons help students use what they know about point of view in real life and apply it to what they read. When you teach Point of View with informational text, you teach students to identify, describe, and explain how an author uses reasons and evidence to support particular points in a text. Beginning in third grade, the Common Core requires students to support their conclusions with evidence from the content or style of the text. Point of View lessons teach students to write opinion pieces comparing their point of view to those of authors, characters, or narrators in texts they have read. Producing opinion pieces that contrast the student's point of view

TIP

In most schools, Point of View is a lesson framework for all students beginning in spring of second grade. First graders can begin to understand point of view by thinking about who is telling the story at various points in the text.

with that of a narrator, character, or author can make an important contribution to the routine writing the Common Core expects all students to do.

Because point of view operates so differently in literature and informational text, we present two sample lessons for this lesson framework, one with each kind of text. The sample lesson for literary text is presented first because it is easier to introduce students to the concept of point of view using characters in a story. Using the gradual release of responsibility model of instruction, Point of View combines student trios and teacher-led collaborative conversations to discuss various aspects of the text's content.

A Sample Point of View Lesson for Literature

Knowing who is telling what happened in a story or narrative poem at any point is very helpful for comprehending literary texts. Because this is the first Point of View lesson that Mr. D. has taught this year, he begins by teaching his students what a point of view is.

Purpose Setting

In order to help his students understand the concept of point of view, Mr. D. precedes his first Point of View lesson by having six students act out a skit. In the skit, a student stumbles and drops his tray in the cafeteria causing food, milk, and dishes to fly everywhere. A few other students point and laugh when the tray hits the floor. A friend quickly comes to the aid of the tray dropper and helps him clean it up and get another tray of food. The other members of the class are the audience for the skit.

When the skit ends, Mr. D. asks the audience members to describe what they saw. Students take turns giving a clear description, explaining the accident, the friend who helped, and the other kids in the cafeteria who laughed. Next, Mr. D. asks the two students playing the main characters to explain what happened in the cafeteria as they would to a parent or someone at home. The student who dropped his tray describes what happened using *I* to refer to himself as his character in the skit. After he describes the mess he made, Mr. D. asks how his character felt about the accident. He states that he was embarrassed, particularly when some of the other kids laughed at him. Then, the friend describes what happened using *I* to refer to himself as his character. Mr. D. asks how his character felt after the student dropped his tray, and he says he felt sorry for him, angry at the kids who were laughing, and motivated to take action.

After this short skit is complete, Mr. D. displays the term *point of view* and explains, "Your point of view is the way you see something and how you feel about it. In this skit, we had two main characters. When they described the accident, they used the word *I* because they were characters in the event. Those of you in the audience were not in the story, but you could tell about it because you saw it happen. When you were retelling what happened, you did not use the word *I* because it did not happen to you. You were being storytellers, or *narrators*. To think about point of view in a piece of literature, we must first determine who the narrator is—who is telling the story. Sometimes the narrator is a character in the story but usually not. Once we determine who is telling the story, we can decide how that person feels about what happens during the story."

The class discussion shows the students understand that each character in a story can have a point of view, that the person who is telling a story can have a point of view, and that each person who sees, hears, or reads a story can have a point of view. The class begins to understand that these points of view about a story can be different, so Mr. D. begins the lesson by showing the students the book *Voices in the Park* by Anthony Browne (1998).

"In this book, four characters each describe a visit to the park," he says. "As you will see, they have different points of view."

Mr. D. displays the chart he will fill in for *Voices in the Park* and that the trios will then fill in for their books. (See figure 11.1.)

Point of View Chart for Literature			
Who Is the Narrator?			
Character	How Does the Character Feel?	What Clues Tell You How the Character Feels?	What Is This Character's Point of View?
Compare your point of view to the points of view of these characters.			

Figure 11.1: Point of View chart for literature.

He says, "Usually when we finish reading a story, we answer 'Who is the narrator, the person telling the story?' first. Then, we answer three questions about each important character in the story: 'How does the character feel about what happened?' 'What does the character do and say that gives us clues so we can figure out how he or she feels?' and 'What is the character's point of view?' We are going to record our answers to these questions for *Voices in the Park* on our Point of View chart. Finally, we are going to each decide what our own point of view about the story is."

I Do, and You Watch

Mr. D. explains, "Almost all stories have one narrator, one person who is telling the story. Sometimes the narrator is the author. Sometimes the narrator is a character in the story. *Voices in the Park* is a very unusual story, because it doesn't have just one narrator; it has four! Because it is so unusual, I am going to fill in the first box that asks us who the narrator is. This book has four parts, each one told by a different character who narrates that part."

Mr. D. answers the question, "Who is the narrator?" by writing in that box on the chart. (See figure 11.2, page 108.)

Point of View Chart for Literature			
Who Is the Narrator?	*There are four narrators. Each one is also a character.*		
Character	*How Does the Character Feel?*	*What Clues Tell You How the Character Feels?*	*What Is This Character's Point of View?*
Compare your point of view to the points of view of these characters.			

Figure 11.2: Sample Point of View chart for literature.

He says, "Now, I am going to read the first part of this book to you. Then, I am going to tell you which character is the narrator, the character who is telling the story in this part. Then, I am going to decide how I think this character feels, what clues I used to figure this out, and what I think the point of view of this character is about the visit to the park. Then, I am going to record this information on the chart."

When he has finished reading the first part to the class, Mr. D. thinks out loud as he completes the chart for the character who is the first narrator: "The narrator of this part is clearly Charles's mom. I know that because she says she is going to take her dog and her son for a walk." He jots down *Charles's mom* in the first character cell in the chart. (See figure 11.3.)

Point of View Chart for Literature			
Who Is the Narrator?	*There are four narrators. Each one is also a character.*		
Character	*How Does the Character Feel?*	*What Clues Tell You How the Character Feels?*	*What Is This Character's Point of View?*
Charles's mom			

Figure 11.3: Sample Point of View chart for literature.

"How does Charles's mom feel?" he asks. "I think she feels angry at the other dog her dog plays with and at the girl her son plays with. I know this because she calls the other dog a 'scruffy mongrel' and a 'horrible thing,' and she calls the girl a 'rough-looking child.' When she and Charles walked home, they didn't talk to one another. So what is her point of view about the visit to the park? She thinks it was terrible!" Mr. D. jots down these characteristics in the chart. (See figure 11.4.)

Point of View Chart for Literature			
Who Is the Narrator?	*There are four narrators. Each one is also a character.*		
Character	How Does the Character Feel?	What Clues Tell You How the Character Feels?	What Is This Character's Point of View?
Charles's mom	*angry at other dog and girl*	*calls other dog a "scruffy mongrel" and a "horrible thing"* *calls girl a "rough-looking child"* *They walked home without talking.*	*The visit to the park was terrible.*

Figure 11.4: Sample Point of View chart for literature.

I Do, and You Help

Mr. D. says, "There are three more characters in this story who each tell about the visit to the park: Charles, Smudge (the girl Charles played with), and Smudge's dad. We are going to read how each of them described the visit to the park, and you are going to help me fill in the chart for those characters."

After the class reads each section together, the class uses the narrator, how that character feels, and the clues from the text to decide point of view. Mr. D. records all this information on the chart.

Finally, Mr. D. directs students' attention to the question at the bottom of the chart. Not surprisingly, all the students agree with Charles and Smudge that the visit to the park was either wonderful or awesome! (See figure 11.5, page 110.)

Point of View Chart for Literature			
Who Is the Narrator?	There are four narrators. Each one is also a character.		
Character	How Does the Character Feel?	What Clues Tell You How the Character Feels?	What Is This Character's Point of View?
Charles's mom	angry at other dog and girl	calls other dog a "scruffy mongrel" and a "horrible thing"	The visit to the park was terrible.
Smudge's dad	happy that Smudge and the dog had a good time	says his dog has lots of energy and loves the park Smudge chattered happily all the way home.	The visit to the park was fun.
Charles	pleased that he had made a new friend and the two dogs were friends	says the two dogs raced around like old friends plays on the climbing bars with Smudge hopes Smudge will be there next time he comes	The visit to the park was wonderful.
Smudge	really happy	played on the seesaw with Charles says she felt really, really happy Charles picked a flower for her.	The visit to the park was awesome.
Compare your point of view to the points of view of these characters. All students agree with Charles or Smudge that the visit to the park was wonderful or awesome.			

Figure 11.5: Sample completed Point of View chart for literature.

You Do It Together, and I Help

Next, Mr. D. shows the class three stories and explains, "Each of these stories has at least two characters that have different points of view about the same event. Your trio is going to read one of these stories and fill in the chart by deciding who the narrator is and who the different characters are, and answering the three questions about each character. I want you to create the chart on this large paper with markers, writing big enough so that we can display the chart and compare each other's answers. Don't answer the question comparing your point of view with that of the characters yet. You will do that individually in writing after we have shared the trios' charts for all the stories."

Mr. D. distributes stories, charts, and markers to each group. He gives one copy of the assigned story to the weakest reader in each group and the chart and marker to the most fluent writer.

The students in each trio read their story together and then get to work on making and filling out the chart. Mr. D. encourages them to look back at the story to find evidence that supports their decisions about how characters feel and what their points of view are.

The Class Debriefs

As the trios finish their charts, Mr. D. helps them tape the charts up around the room. He encourages all the students to go around and read the charts of the other trios when they have finished their own chart. The students are particularly interested in comparing their charts with the charts of the other trios who have read the same story.

On the following day, Mr. D. leads the students to review all the trios' Point of View charts that are still hanging around the classroom. Then, he draws their attention to the question at the bottom of the chart.

He says, "You know that this year, we have been working on writing opinion pieces and have written several. When we give our opinion about something we experienced or something we read, we are actually sharing our point of view. Right now, I am going to write an opinion piece comparing my point of view to that of the four characters in *Voices in the Park* and have you watch me do it. After I finish mine, each of you will write an opinion piece comparing your point of view with the points of view of the characters in the story your trio read. When you're done, you'll take turns sharing some of your opinion pieces by reading them aloud."

Mr. D. writes his opinion piece on the board while the students watch.

> The characters in <u>Voices in the Park</u> all visited the park at the same time, but they had different points of view about the visit. My point of view is a lot like the points of view of the kids. They played together on the equipment, and I think Charles and Smudge might meet at the park again and become friends. I thought the visit was wonderful and awesome. I think Charles's mom was just being grumpy or having a bad

TIP

Assign students to trios so each trio contains a variety of abilities. Designate the struggling reader to sit in the middle and hold the story. Have the most fluent writer be the recorder.

day and didn't think about the fact that the dogs and kids were all having a good time.

The students clearly pay attention while Mr. D. writes because a few students mumble-read as he writes and others whisper comments to their neighbor. When he finishes, he asks them what they think about his opinion, and most of them speak or nod in agreement. Next, the students write opinion pieces comparing their points of view with those of the characters in the story they read in their trios. Before they write, Mr. D. reminds them to support their opinions with good reasons, such as in the third column of their trio's Point of View chart. After students have written their summary, Mr. D. has one student from each trio volunteer to read his or her opinion piece to the class. The class has a brief discussion about each opinion piece shared.

A Sample Point of View Lesson for Informational Text

Of the ten Common Core Reading anchor standards, the greatest difference in the application between literature and informational text is in standard six (CCRA.R.6). Even when students have become quite comfortable with identifying the point of view of a narrator or character in literature and contrasting it with their own, they may still have difficulty discerning the author's purpose and point of view implicit in an informational text. Consequently, Mr. D. takes little for granted as he begins teaching his students to comprehend author's purpose and point of view when reading expository text.

Purpose Setting

Mr. D. says, "From time to time this year, we have worked with the Point of View chart for stories. In each of those lessons, you read a story in your trio and then completed the chart by writing answers to the questions. Afterward, we shared and discussed how trios answered the questions for the same story. Today, we're going to begin working with a similar chart for informational texts."

Mr. D. displays the new chart. (See figure 11.6.)

Mr. D. briefly explains what each of the questions on the chart asks students to do. Then, he holds up a past issue of a magazine for children. He turns to an article in it and reads the title of the article and who wrote it. He asks them, "Have any of you seen the Disney movie *Finding Nemo*?"

Several students have, and there is an enthusiastic discussion about the movie.

Soon, Mr. D. continues, "As some of you know, Nemo in that movie is a clown fish. I want you to listen as I read this magazine article because it is about clown fish."

I Do, and You Watch

Mr. D. reads the article aloud and shows them the pictures. He says, "Now, I am going to think of answers to the first two questions and write them on the chart."

Although he planned this lesson the evening before, he pretends to deliberate for several seconds, then thinks out loud, "I don't think the main thing the author was trying to do was to entertain us or make us laugh or cry. And I don't think the author's main purpose was to persuade us or convince us to believe something or do something. No, I think the author's general purpose for writing this article was to inform us, to teach us."

Point of View Chart for Informational Texts		
What Is the Author's General Purpose for Writing This Text?		
What Is the Author's Point of View?		
A Main Point the Author Is Making	*What Reasons Does the Author Give to Support This Point?*	*What Evidence Does the Author Give to Support This Point?*
Compare your point of view to the point of view of the author.		

Figure 11.6: Point of View chart for informational texts.

He writes *To teach us* after "What is the author's general purpose for writing this text?" on the chart. Then, he pretends to reflect again. Momentarily, he thinks aloud, "The author doesn't express a clear point of view, but I believe I can guess what that point of view is. I think the author wants clown fish to be protected under the Endangered Species Act." He also writes that on the chart.

I Do, and You Help

Mr. D. says, "I want you to help me decide the main points the author made in the article. For each main point, we'll decide what reasons or evidence the author gave us to support it. Do any of you think you know what one of the main points was?"

A few students reluctantly raise their hands. The first one he calls on suggests that it is a main point that clown fish are in danger. When several students nod and Mr. D. agrees, he writes that answer on the chart. He uses the word *species* when he writes, because it is a science vocabulary word they have been using this year. He continues asking the students to help him fill in the chart. He tells them they can ask him to reread a part from the article to help them.

The task is quite difficult for them, and he monitors how many students are actually helping him by asking him to reread something or making a suggestion about what he can write in a cell. He decides that about one-third are helping, another third are paying good attention, but the last third are lost. From this formative assessment, he knows he will need to repeat the "I do, and you watch" and "I do, and you help" phases of his Point of View lessons for informational texts for the foreseeable future. Finally, together the class completes the chart except for the bottom box. He saves this for the class debrief. (See figure 11.7, page 114.)

Point of View Chart for Informational Texts		
What Is the Author's General Purpose for Writing This Text?	*to teach us*	
What Is the Author's Point of View?	*for clown fish to be protected under the Endangered Species Act*	
A Main Point the Author Is Making	*What Reasons Does the Author Give to Support This Point?*	*What Evidence Does the Author Give to Support This Point?*
The clown fish species is in danger.	*A number of environmentalists say so.*	*The Center for Biological Diversity filed a petition with the National Marine Fisheries Service to add clown fish to the list of endangered species.*
Coral reefs, clown fishes' habitat, are in danger.	*Many marine biologists say the reefs are slowly dying.*	*Dr. Shaye Wolf, a biologist and ecologist in California, says coral reefs are becoming unhealthy.*
Compare your point of view to the point of view of the author.		

Figure 11.7: Sample completed Point of View chart for informational texts.

You Do It Together, and I Help

The next day, Mr. D. holds up three texts and explains to the class, "Yesterday, you helped me fill out our new Point of View chart for informational texts with answers we figured out from the article about clown fish. Today, I want you to work in trios to complete the chart for an informational text you read."

In preparation for this part of the Point of View lesson, Mr. D. searched through his materials and asked for the media specialist's help to find three short articles about endangered species that would be as easy as possible for his students to read. Later, when his students are better at determining point of view for informational texts, he will select more grade-appropriate texts.

The students move into their trios, and Mr. D. distributes one copy of the Point of View chart for informational texts and one copy of an article on an endangered species to each trio. Mr. D. walks around and helps the trios when they ask for it or seem to need it. He reminds them to return to the article they have read to help them decide what to write on their chart.

The Class Debriefs

As the trios complete their charts, Mr. D. quickly eyeballs them. If he thinks a trio has made a good effort, he helps the students tape their chart up somewhere around the room. He encourages students to walk around and read the charts of the other trios after they have finished their own chart. Mr. D. finishes this part of the lesson by leading a discussion of differences in the charts on the same article.

On the third day, Mr. D. again has the students quickly review all the trios' Point of View charts hanging around the classroom. Then, he draws their attention to the question at the bottom of the chart. He says he is going to write an opinion piece while the students watch. He displays the chart on clown fish they helped him complete two days before. He tells them, "My job in this piece is to compare my point of view with the author's."

The author's point of view in this article is that the United States should add clown fish to its endangered species list. I'm not so sure. It would be all right with me for clown fish to be on the list, but I think coral reefs are the problem. Maybe the United States also needs an endangered places list. Then, coral reefs could be on it. That might help both coral reefs and clown fish!

After Mr. D. finishes writing, he reads his opinion piece aloud to the class, and a lively discussion ensues. He is pleased to see that most of his students have a definite point of view about what, if anything, should be done about clown fish and understand that their point of view could and perhaps did differ from the author's or from his.

Then, each student writes an opinion piece about the article read in his or her trio. He tells students to refer to their trios' charts taped up around the room. As they write, he walks around to help them if they ask for it, but as they knew he would, he refuses to spell words for them or answer questions about any other mechanics or usage conventions. Otherwise, he'd take up class time on spelling and conventions issues instead of on author's point of view.

Mr. D. is satisfied with the three days he spends with his first Point of View lesson for informational text. He knows that future lessons will take less time and is confident that eventually almost all of his students will make progress on comprehending the author's purpose and point of view implicit in an informational text as well as determining what reasons and evidence the author gave to support the points he or she was making.

Planning and Teaching a Point of View Lesson

More than the other lesson frameworks in this book, vary Point of View lessons depending on whether the one you are planning is the first, third, fifth, or whichever. There are two reasons for this. First, students have opinions—points of view—about almost everything, but their *awareness* of point of view is quite abstract. Second, students generally find it easier to understand the point of view of a character in a literary text than that of the author of an informational text.

Therefore, you should introduce the concept of *point of view* in the first lesson or two by having a few students act out a common school event, where actors have different feelings and understandings about the situation. After the skit, characters pretend to describe what happened to someone who didn't witness it. Have members of the audience for the skit tell what happened and make clear that they are being narrators when they are telling the story. Use the skit to help students understand what narrators do and that characters can have different points of view.

For the first several Point of View lessons, choose a literary text in which different characters clearly have different points of view. Use one of these stories for the "I do, and you watch" and "I do, and you help" phases of a lesson. Have students watch you and then help you complete the Point of View chart for stories by deciding on answers to the questions on the chart. Students enjoy thinking about point of view by comparing different versions of familiar stories such as *The Three Little Pigs* and *The True Story of the Three Little Pigs*, which is told from the wolf's point of view. Steck Vaughn has a series of point of view stories in which the same book includes two versions of the story. (The comparison of *Rumpelstiltskin* and *A Deal Is a Deal* told by Rumpelstiltskin is hilarious!) Also, for each of these first several lessons, choose three or four stories for the trios to read and work with in which two or more characters have different points of view.

Eventually, students will be ready for Point of View lessons for informational texts. As with literature, your first several lessons with informational text should include the "I do, and you watch" and "I do, and you help" phases. Students watch you and then help you complete the Point of View chart for informational texts by providing answers to the questions on the chart. Again, in these lessons, you would choose three or four informational texts in which the author has a clear point of view for student trios to read and use to complete the chart. Use the following six steps when teaching a Point of View lesson.

1. Establish the purpose for the lesson. Depending on whether the lesson is for literary or informational text, display the appropriate chart and discuss the questions on it. Explain to the students that they will learn how to fill in the chart for this kind of text (either a story or an informational text) by figuring out answers to the questions.

2. For the first several lessons with each kind of text, be sure to include the "I do, and you watch" and "I do, and you help" phases of the lesson. Have students first watch and then help you answer the questions on the chart.

3. In each lesson, organize trios with students of different reading and writing abilities. Give each trio one copy of the text you have chosen and designate who will do the writing on the chart and who will sit in the middle and

hold the text ("You do it together, and I help"). Help by circulating, coaching, and formatively assessing how the students are interacting in their trios. Coach students to keep returning to their text to find specific clues, reasoning, or evidence for questions on their chart.

4. Have the class debrief by asking trios to share their completed charts and discussing differences among charts for the same text.

5. Model writing an opinion piece in which you compare your point of view with that of the characters or author, depending on the kind of text.

6. Have students write opinion pieces in which they compare their point of view with that of characters in their story or the author of their informational text. Share these opinion pieces, and discuss students' different points of view.

Point of View Lessons Across the Year

In subsequent lessons as students demonstrate their ability to determine point of view and compare their points of view to those of others, fade out the modeling and guidance you provide. When your observations of the trios' interactions indicate that most of your students have learned to determine and compare points of view, give them a text to read, and have them complete the appropriate Point of View chart independently ("You do, and I watch"). Don't be surprised if students require lots of work with this lesson framework before they achieve an independent level. Determining and comparing points of view requires a high level of abstract thinking.

The jargon for telling a story when you are a narrator but not a character is *third-person narration*. When the character tells the story and uses the word *I*, it is *first-person narration*. You can decide whether and when your students need to learn these distinctions and terms. We find that such jargon is much easier to learn after students are able to complete Point of View charts for literature.

To help students apply their point of view skills when reading on their own, remind students as they are about to begin their independent reading time that they should think about the point of view of the author or characters and compare it to their own. When the independent reading time is over, take a few minutes to let volunteers share what they determined about the author's or character's point of view and compare it with their own point of view.

How Point of View Lessons Teach the Standards

The Point of View lesson framework teaches Reading anchor standard six (CCRA.R.6), because its main purpose is to help students learn to ascertain the point of view of authors, characters, or narrators from the content or style of the text. It also helps students meet Reading informational text standard eight (RI.8), because students identify and describe particular points the author is making in a text. The lessons help students meet Reading anchor standard one (CCRA.R.1), because they learn to read closely to discover the point of view of authors, characters, or narrators. Point of View lessons teach Writing anchor standard one (CCRA.W.1), because students write opinion pieces comparing their point of view to those of authors, characters, or narrators in texts they have read. They teach Writing anchor standard ten (CCRA.W.10), because the opinion pieces students produce make a contribution to the routine writing the Common Core expects all students to do. The lessons teach Speaking and Listening anchor standard one (CCRA.SL.1), because they engage students in collaborative conversations on texts with peers in their trios as well as their teacher and peers during group instruction.

CCSS in a Poetry Aloud Lesson

Poetry Aloud is a lesson framework that helps students comprehend text and differentiate poetry from other genres. When you lead students through this lesson several times, you are helping them learn the reading and language skills in the following standards.

Reading

CCRA.R.1: Read closely to determine what the text says explicitly and to make logical inferences from it; cite specific textual evidence when writing or speaking to support conclusions drawn from the text.

CCRA.R.4: Interpret words and phrases as they are used in a text, including determining technical, connotative, and figurative meanings, and analyze how specific word choices shape meaning or tone.

RL.3.5: Refer to parts of stories, dramas, and poems when writing or speaking about a text, using terms such as *chapter*, *scene*, and *stanza*; describe how each successive part builds on earlier sections.

RL.4.5: Explain major differences between poems, drama, and prose, and refer to the structural elements of poems (such as verse, rhythm, and meter) and drama (such as casts of characters, settings, descriptions, dialogue, and stage directions) when writing or speaking about a text.

RL.5.5: Explain how a series of chapters, scenes, or stanzas fits together to provide the overall structure of a particular story, drama, or poem.

RF.1–2.4b: Read grade-level text orally with accuracy, appropriate rate, and expression on successive readings.

RF.3–5.4b: Read grade-level prose and poetry orally with accuracy, appropriate rate, and expression on successive readings.

Language

CCRA.L.4: Determine or clarify the meaning of unknown and multiple-meaning words and phrases by using context clues, analyzing meaningful word parts, and consulting general and specialized reference materials, as appropriate.

CCRA.L.5: Demonstrate understanding of figurative language, word relationships, and nuances in word meanings.

Source: Adapted from NGA & CCSSO, 2010, pp. 10, 12, 15, 25.

CHAPTER 12

Poetry Aloud

Most of the comprehension lesson frameworks in this book help students build strategies for comprehending text when they are reading silently. Learning to read aloud with phrasing and expression is also an important goal and helps students develop fluency and confidence. Plays and poetry are the obvious media for reading aloud. Much of the enjoyment of poetry comes from the way it sounds—the rhythm, rhyme, repeated sounds, words, and phrases. As students reread verses of poems to get the phrasing just right, they are getting the repeated reading practice they need to develop reading fluency.

Poetry usually contains words and phrases that are unfamiliar to your students or are used in a different way than they're used to. Poetry provides you with a wonderful opportunity to work with all your students to help them develop word meanings and interpret figurative language. Understanding poetry requires students to analyze what the poem is saying. When you lead them in a stanza-by-stanza discussion, you help them pay attention to what the text says and figure out what it means. Reading poems several times during the echo and choral reading parts of the lesson helps students learn to read with accuracy, appropriate rate, and expression.

There are many wonderful poems you can use with students. You can access these poems in books and on the Internet. You can find poems that tie in with your science and social studies units, and there are also wonderful poems to help students learn and practice mathematics concepts. For this lesson framework, we chose three poems that are in the public domain so we could show examples of how you can use poetry to build a variety of skills.

The Poetry Aloud lesson framework leads students through a sequence of activities that will help them learn to enjoy and interpret poetry and engage in meaningful repeated reading. This lesson framework works primarily on fluency and, unlike the comprehension and writing lesson frameworks in this book, does not fit well with the gradual release of responsibility framework.

TIP

You can find poems appropriate for students of all ages from kindergarten on up. Most older students should read silently, but poetry provides a nice change of pace and gives them a real purpose to practice their oral reading skills.

A Sample Poetry Aloud Lesson

Friday is a special day in Miss L.'s classroom. On Fridays, her class reads poetry or plays, many of which she finds on the Internet. Early in the year, she teaches her students rhymes and chants. Later, she uses poems and plays that connect to topics the class is studying in mathematics, science, and social studies. Miss L.'s class even celebrates holidays with plays and poetry. Each student has an anthology binder to store his or her copies of the plays and poems. On Friday afternoon, the students take their binder home. For weekend homework, they read new plays or poetry and some of their old favorites to an appreciative audience. Often on Friday afternoon, Miss L. arranges to take her students to a kindergarten class where they perform their plays and poetry. This is the first Poetry Aloud lesson, and Miss L. has chosen three animal poems, two of which, "The Itsy Bitsy Spider" and "Five Little Monkeys," students are familiar with and one of which, "The Squirrel," is new to them.

She has made copies of all three poems and left space on the copy for students to illustrate the poems if they choose. For each poem, she leads students through both echo reading and choral reading, so each student reads the poem several times. Next, she helps her students build meanings for any unfamiliar words or familiar words the story uses in a different way. Finally, they complete some word activities.

"The Itsy Bitsy Spider"

First, Miss L. focuses on the song "The Itsy Bitsy Spider." Students are all familiar with this song and know actions to do with the words. Before giving them the printed copy, Miss L. sings the song and does the familiar actions. Then, she hands everyone a sheet with the song.

She says, "'The Itsy Bitsy Spider' is both a song and a poem. We can sing the song as we just did, and we can read the poem. Now we are going to focus on reading the poem. We are going to first do an echo reading of the poem. Who knows what an echo is?"

Several students know what an echo is, and she has them say something and then tell what the echo sounds like. Most of her students, however, do not understand what an echo is. Miss L. has anticipated this and searches YouTube for a quick video that demonstrates an echo and explains that an echo is a repeated sound that reflects off of a surface.

Once her students have heard the echoes on the video, they are all eager to try to be her echo. She draws their attention to the first line of the poem and reads it with expression: "The itsy bitsy spider went up the waterspout."

The students read it back, trying to sound like her echo.

She continues reading the poem one line at a time and then waits for the students to echo it back.

She leads them through one more quick echo reading, and they are more fluent and expressive on this second reading.

Before going on to choral reading, she helps students clarify meaning for any unfamiliar words and phrases. In this short poem, the only words she needs to build meaning for are *itsy bitsy* and *waterspout*. She draws students' attention to the first line of the poem and asks them what *itsy bitsy* means. Some students explain that it means *really*

TIP

During echo reading, model expressive reading so your students try to sound just like you—like your echo. If your students don't know what an echo sounds like, they will not understand this activity. Fortunately, there are several short videos on the Internet that demonstrate echoes!

little. Next, she asks them what a waterspout is and leads them to understand that it is the downspout that directs rain off of a roof. Some students are still confused, and she promises they'll check out the waterspouts on the school during recess.

For the choral reading, she divides the class into four groups. She then assigns each group one of the four lines in the poem. Students gather together and practice their line once, and she leads them to read the poem chorally—with each group reading its line together. The class repeats this choral reading three more times, rotating which group reads which line until all groups have chorally read each of the lines. Finally, the whole class reads the whole poem chorally, and Miss L. observes that even her struggling readers read accurately, confidently, and expressively.

"Five Little Monkeys"

Second, Miss L. focuses on "The Five Little Monkeys." Students are all familiar with this song. Before giving them the printed copy, Miss L. sings the song. Then, she hands everyone a sheet with the song.

She uses echo reading for the first reading of this poem, reading the poem one line at a time for the first echo reading and then two lines at a time for the second echo reading.

Since there are no unfamiliar words to build concepts for, she proceeds directly to choral reading. She points out that this poem has four stanzas and has the students count off to arrange themselves into four groups. She assigns stanzas to the groups, and they practice reading the poem together before reading it chorally. The groups then perform the choral reading for the class, and she assigns each group a different stanza. She continues this until every group has practiced and performed every stanza. Students finish working with this poem by doing a whole-class choral reading, and again she notices all her students reading accurately, confidently, and expressively.

"The Squirrel"

Lastly, Miss L. focuses on the animal poem "The Squirrel," which students are not familiar with. Using the same strategies she used for the first two poems, she reads the poem to the students before giving them a printed copy.

She hands each student a copy of "The Squirrel" and leads them in an echo reading of each stanza.

The Squirrel

Whisky, frisky, hippity hop,
Up he goes to the treetop.

Whirly, twirly, round and round,
Down he scampers to the ground.

Furly, curly, what a tail!
Tall as a feather, broad as a sail!

Where's his supper? In the shell.
Snappity, crackity—out it fell!

The poem contains lots of unfamiliar words, so after the echo reading, she leads students to describe what is happening in each stanza.

In the first stanza, the squirrel is going up a tree. She asks her students if they have ever seen a squirrel going up a tree and how it climbs. There are lots of squirrels in the school's neighborhood, so it is not hard for students to describe how squirrels climb.

One student says, "They climb so fast, it almost looks like they are flying."

Miss L. shows them how the rhyming words *whisky* and *frisky* help them picture how fast the squirrel is climbing.

The second stanza describes how he comes down the tree. The words *whirly, twirly,* and *scampers* help students visualize his descent.

The third stanza compares the *furly, curly tail* to a feather and a sail. Miss L. asks her students to show with their hands how tall and broad the tail is. Many students are unfamiliar with the meaning of the word *broad*. Miss L. helps them understand that since *tall* refers to the height of the feather, *broad* must refer to its width.

The final stanza is a bit cryptic, but Miss L. leads students to figure out that he has found a nut and has them imagine the *snappity, crackity* sound it makes when he cracks it with his sharp teeth.

Before proceeding to choral reading, Miss L. helps her students analyze the form of the poem. They count the four stanzas. In addition to the rhyming words within the sentences, she helps them notice that the last word of the first line and the last word of the second line of each stanza rhyme. They identify and pronounce the rhyming words—*hop, top; round, ground; tail, sail; shell, fell.*

They finish their work with "The Squirrel" with choral reading. The students count off by fours and arrange themselves with their groups. They then read the poem chorally four times, alternating which group begins the reading each time and making sure everyone gets to read each stanza. For the final choral reading, the whole class reads the whole poem.

The Class Debriefs

Miss L. always creates activities that focus student attention on the individual words in poems, especially when students are unfamiliar with them. Because they were not familiar with "The Squirrel," she focuses her activities on words in this poem. Students put copies of each poem in their anthology and then complete two activities that focus their attention on rhymes and nouns. Miss L. circulates and encourages them to look back at the poem if they need to. (See figure 12.1, and see figure 12.2, page 126.)

Planning and Teaching a Poetry Aloud Lesson

Find poems that will appeal to your students and that most students will be able to read independently and fluently after engaging in the echo and choral readings. When possible, choose a poem that connects to a holiday or a mathematics, science, or social studies unit you are working on. Decide what vocabulary and inferences you will need to help your students figure out so that they can understand and enjoy the poem. Decide what elements of the poem—rhyme, alliteration, simile, metaphor, or

TIP

If your students are unfamiliar with squirrels, show them a quick video from YouTube.

Rhymes

Directions: Someone took these rhyming words out of the poem. Can you put them back where they go?

frisky   ground   hop   twirly   curly   sail   fell

Whisky, _____,
Hippity _____,
Up he goes
To the treetop!

Whirly, _____,
Round and round,
Down he scampers
To the _____.

Furly, _____,
What a tail!
Tall as a feather,
Broad as a _____!

Where's his supper?
In the shell,
Snappity, crackity—
Out it _____!

Figure 12.1: Sample word activity on rhymes.

form—you want your students to notice. Use the following eight steps when teaching a Poetry Aloud lesson.

1. Display the poem so that everyone can see it or give everyone an individual copy. If the poem is one your students know, have them sing or recite it before drawing their attention to the printed copy.

2. Lead the students in an echo reading of the poem. For the first several lessons or for poems with long lines or long stanzas, conduct echo reading line by line. Have students echo your voice line by line or stanza by stanza. Remind your students that that an echo sounds exactly like the voice it is echoing.

3. Lead your students to talk about what each stanza of the poem says. Poems require a lot of inferencing. They seldom state facts in a literal way. Have your students figure out what each stanza means and explain how they figured it out.

Nouns

Directions: Someone took these nouns out of the poem. Can you put them back where they go?

ground   treetop   sail   feather   tail   shell

Whisky, frisky,
Hippity hop,
Up he goes
To the _____!

Whirly, twirly,
Round and round,
Down he scampers
To the _____.

Furly, curly,
What a _____!
Tall as a _____,
Broad as a _____!

Where's his supper?
In the _____,
Snappity, crackity—
Out it fell!

Figure 12.2: Sample word activity on rhymes.

4. Help students build and clarify meanings for unfamiliar words or familiar words the poem uses in a different way.

5. Have students notice distinctive features of the poem and use appropriate words—*stanzas, rhyme, alliteration, simile, metaphor,* and so on—to describe the poem.

6. Have students count off according to the number of lines or stanzas and arrange themselves together by number. Have each group practice and then chorally read one stanza of the poem. Continue the choral reading until every group has had a chance to read every stanza. Finish by having the whole class do a choral reading of the whole poem.

7. Have students complete some activities to focus their attention on some of the words.

8. If your students are creating personal poetry or play anthologies, have them place the pieces in their notebooks. Let them add illustrations if they choose. Have them take their anthologies home and read the new poems

and old favorites to family, friends, and neighbors. Periodically, arrange for your class to perform some of their plays and poems for other classes in your school.

Poetry Aloud Lessons Across the Year

Continue to include Poetry Aloud lessons throughout the year to provide students with opportunities for meaningful repeated readings. Elementary students need constant practice reading aloud to learn to read with fluency, accuracy, and appropriate expression. When almost all students understand poetry features, have students choose poems to read. Use these assessments to determine which students need more instruction on certain features.

How Poetry Aloud Lessons Teach the Standards

The Poetry Aloud lesson framework teaches Reading Foundational Skills standard four (RF.4b), because as students engage in repeated readings of poetry, they become fluent readers who read with accuracy, appropriate rate, and expression. Poetry Aloud lessons help students meet Reading anchor standards one and four (CCRA.R.1 and CCRA.R.4) because students learn to read closely and make inferences to interpret the poems and the words and phrases in the poem to determine figurative meanings. This focus on word meanings, including figurative language, also helps students meet Language anchor standards four and five (CCRA.L.4 and CCRA.L.5). When you focus students' attention on the distinctive features of poetry, you are helping them meet Reading literature standard five (RL.5), which specifies that students should be able to explain major differences between poems, drama, and prose, and a poem's structural elements.

CCSS in a Plays Aloud Lesson

Plays Aloud is a lesson framework to help students build fluency with a focus on expressive reading. When you lead students through this lesson several times, you are helping them learn the reading skills in the following standards.

Reading

CCRA.R.1: Read closely to determine what the text says explicitly and to make logical inferences from it; cite specific textual evidence when writing or speaking to support conclusions drawn from the text.

CCRA.R.4: Interpret words and phrases as they are used in a text, including determining technical, connotative, and figurative meanings, and analyze how specific word choices shape meaning or tone.

RL.3.5: Refer to parts of stories, dramas, and poems when writing or speaking about a text, using terms such as *chapter*, *scene*, and *stanza*; describe how each successive part builds on earlier sections.

RL.4.5: Explain major differences between poems, drama, and prose, and refer to the structural elements of poems (such as verse, rhythm, and meter) and drama (such as casts of characters, settings, descriptions, dialogue, and stage directions) when writing or speaking about a text.

RL.5.5: Explain how a series of chapters, scenes, or stanzas fits together to provide the overall structure of a particular story, drama, or poem.

RF.1–2.4b: Read grade-level text orally with accuracy, appropriate rate, and expression on successive readings.

RF.3–5.4b: Read grade-level prose and poetry orally with accuracy, appropriate rate, and expression on successive readings.

Source: Adapted from NGA & CCSSO, 2010, pp. 10, 12, 15–17.

CHAPTER 13

Plays Aloud

Students love plays, and you can capitalize on their affinity for them and provide repeated reading practice required to build reading fluency and self-confidence. Plays Aloud lessons also help students understand how to read drama and differentiate it from other genres. As you lead students to analyze characters' emotions and read lines with appropriate expression, you are teaching them how to infer characters' feelings and motivations. As with the Poetry Aloud lesson framework in chapter 12, Plays Aloud builds fluency with a focus on expressive reading. This lesson framework also begins with echo reading and then moves to choral reading.

Reading plays several times during the echo and choral reading parts of the lessons helps students learn to read with accuracy, appropriate rate, and expression. After the echo reading, students summarize what happens in each scene, and the teacher clarifies unfamiliar words and phrases. Summarizing what happens in each scene helps students pay attention to what is happening in each part of the play.

A Sample Plays Aloud Lesson

For this sample lesson, we will return to Miss L.'s classroom. On this Friday, Miss L. has planned a Plays Aloud lesson. This is the first Plays Aloud lesson her class has experienced, but having participated in two Poetry Aloud lessons, students are all familiar with echo and choral reading. Echo and choral reading help students learn to read with accuracy, fluency, and appropriate expression. She chooses plays that fit into the units she is working on in science and social studies and always celebrates holidays with plays.

Since this is her students' first Plays Aloud lesson, Miss L. wants to use a play that is not too long or complex. She decides to rewrite a familiar story, "The Little Red Hen," in play format and divide it into five scenes. She reads the play to students, using different voices for each character and lots of expression.

TIP

See chapter 12, page 122, for how to teach students what an echo sounds like.

The Little Red Hen

Characters: little red hen, dog, cat, and duck

Scene One

Narrator: Once upon a time, a dog, a cat, a duck, and a little red hen all lived together on a farm. One day, the little red hen found a grain of wheat. She decided to plant the wheat, and she asked her friends to help.

Little Red Hen: Good morning, friends. Look at the grain of wheat I found. I am going to plant it and grow a wheat plant. Who will help me plant the wheat?

Narrator: The dog and the cat and the duck were all running around playing, and they didn't want to stop playing to help.

Dog: Not I!

Cat: Not I!

Duck: Not I!

Little Red Hen: Well then, I will just plant it myself!

Scene Two

Narrator: In a few weeks, the wheat grain grew into a big plant. The little red hen asked her friends to help her harvest the wheat.

Little Red Hen: Good morning, friends. Look at the tall wheat plant. Who will help me harvest the wheat?

Dog: Not I!

Cat: Not I!

Duck: Not I!

Little Red Hen: Well then, I will just harvest it myself!

Scene Three

Narrator: After she harvested the wheat, the little red hen needed to take it to the mill to be ground into flour.

Little Red Hen: Good morning, friends. I am going to the mill to get the wheat ground into flour. Who will help me carry the wheat?

Dog: Not I!

Cat: Not I!

Duck: Not I!

Little Red Hen: Well then, I will just carry it to the mill myself!

Scene Four

Narrator: The little red hen came back with a sack of flour. She asked her friends for help again.

Little Red Hen: Good afternoon, friends. I am going to bake bread with this flour. Who will help me bake the bread?

Dog: Not I!

Cat: Not I!

Duck: Not I!

Little Red Hen: Well then, I will just bake it myself!

Scene Five

Narrator: The little red hen made the bread and put it in the oven to bake. When the bread was done, she took it outside to show her friends.

Little Red Hen: Good evening, friends. Look at this beautiful loaf of bread. Who will help me eat this bread?

Dog: I will!

Cat: I will!

Duck: I will!

Little Red Hen: I don't think so. I did all the work, and you wouldn't help me. My baby chicks and I are going to eat all this bread.

Narrator: The dog, cat, and duck were very sad, and they decided that the next time the little red hen asked for help, they would help her so they could share in what she made.

Echo Reading the Play

Miss L. gives each student a copy of the play and tells students that they are going to echo read the play just as they do for the poems. She tells them that they are going to read the whole play first and reminds them that the echo needs to sound just like her voice. They read the play together with the whole class echoing Miss L.'s voice. As before, she changes her voice for each character. The students delight in reading in the voices of the dog, cat, duck, hen, and narrator. For the first echo reading, she reads one sentence at a time. They then do a second echo reading, and she reads the whole part for each character.

Focusing on Characters and Summarizing the Scenes

After echo reading the play, Miss L. draws her students' attention to the form of the play. This play has a narrator and four characters. She helps them understand that the narrator tells what is happening but is not really a character in the play. She helps them think about what each character is feeling and has them reread some of the lines to show the emotion by the way they say the words.

Next, she draws their attention to the different scenes and helps students notice that the scenes happen at different times. The scenes in a play show the order or sequence in which the action takes place. She draws a simple timeline (see figure 13.1) on the board and has students summarize what happens in each scene. She writes their summary next to the appropriate scene. As she helps them summarize each scene, she builds meanings for unfamiliar words or phrases. For this simple play, the concepts some of her students may not be familiar with are *harvest*, *mill*, and *ground into flour*.

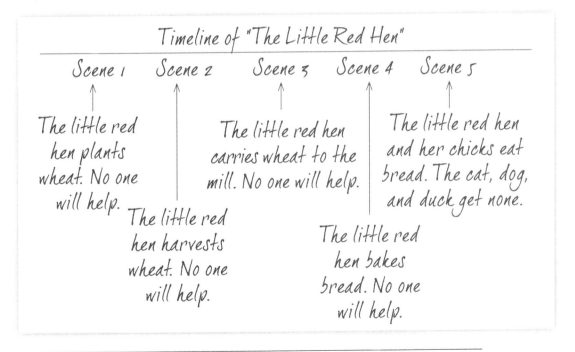

Figure 13.1: Sample timeline summarizing "The Little Red Hen."

Choral Reading

For the choral reading, she arranges her students into five groups, making sure to have some able readers and some struggling readers in each group. She gives each student a sticky note on which she has written the role he or she will have in the play. She assigns more able readers to the role of the narrator and the little red hen and less able readers to the roles of the cat, dog, and duck.

TIP

If your groups don't divide evenly, distribute roles across the groups, and have two students in a group play the same role.

The groups practice the play together twice, with each student reading his or her assigned part. Miss L. circulates among students and formatively assesses each group. Then, she assembles the class for a choral reading. For this reading, students get together with the other students who have the same part. They then do a choral reading of the play—with each group reading its assigned part.

The Class Debriefs

The students put the play in their binders along with the poems they read earlier. Miss L. reminds them of their weekend homework—to read the play to family, friends, or neighbors. Several students comment that this is their favorite homework. One student says he plans to have his family members read the different parts of the play and do the different voices. Other students like his idea and want to do the same.

Planning and Teaching a Plays Aloud Lesson

Choose a play that your students will enjoy doing and that has several characters and a narrator. If the play does not designate the scenes, you may want to divide the play into scenes. Decide which words and phrases your students may be unfamiliar with and which you will need to help them build meanings for after the initial echo reading.

Older students enjoy reading plays, and it gives them a chance to practice their oral reading skills. You can find readers' theater scripts online that connect to your social studies topics. For example, Scholastic (www.scholastic.com/teachers/unit/readers -theater-everything-you-need) offers scripts, tips, props, and guidelines you can use with Plays Aloud lessons. (The script on Harriet Tubman is wonderful!) Use the following six steps when teaching a Plays Aloud lesson.

1. Read the play to students, using a different voice for each character. Then, display a copy of the text where everyone can see, or give everyone an individual copy.

2. Lead the students in an echo reading of the play. Depending on the age of your students and the lengths of the sentences and parts, you may want to do the echo reading sentence by sentence or part by part.

3. After the echo reading, lead your students in a discussion of the play. Have them identify what the narrators and characters do and say. Talk about how the characters are feeling and have them reread the characters' lines with expression that shows that emotion.

4. Draw attention to the scenes in the play and what is happening in each scene. Help students build and clarify meanings for unfamiliar words or phrases as you talk about each scene. Draw a timeline, and help students

construct a brief summary of what is happening in each scene. This visual display helps students see that a scene shows a change in the time or place of the action.

5. Put students in groups to read the play together. Designate which role each student should read, giving longer parts to more able readers and shorter parts to less able readers. Have the groups read the play together twice to rehearse for the whole-class choral performance.

6. Assemble the class, and group the students who have the same roles together. Have them read the play, with all the students assigned the same role reading that part chorally.

Plays Aloud Lessons Across the Year

Continue to include Plays Aloud lessons throughout the year to provide students with opportunities for meaningful repeated readings. Elementary students need constant practice reading aloud to learn to read with fluency, accuracy, and appropriate expression. Have students choose plays to read during independent reading time. Use these assessments to determine which students need more instruction on certain features.

How Plays Aloud Lessons Teach the Standards

The Plays Aloud lesson framework teaches Reading Foundational Skills standard four (RF.4b) because as students engage in repeated readings of plays, they become fluent readers who read with accuracy, appropriate rate, and expression. Plays Aloud lessons help students meet Reading anchor standards one and four (CCRA.R.1 and CCRA.R.4) because students learn to read closely and make inferences to interpret the poems and to interpret words and phrases in the plays. When you focus students' attention on the distinctive features of plays, you are helping them meet Reading literature standard five (RL.5), which specifies that students should be able to explain major differences between poems, drama, and prose, and the structural elements of plays.

CCSS in a Word Detectives Lesson

Word Detectives is a lesson framework that teaches students how to use context, visuals, and morphemic clues to figure out appropriate meanings for words they encounter in narrative or informational text. When you lead students through this lesson several times and gradually release responsibility to them, you are helping them learn the reading, speaking and listening, and language skills in the following standards.

Reading

RI.2.4: Determine the meaning of words and phrases in a text relevant to a *grade 2 topic or subject area.*

RI.3–5.4: Determine the meaning of general academic and domain-specific words or phrases in a text relevant to a *grade-level topic or subject area.*

Speaking and Listening

CCRA.SL.1: Prepare for and participate effectively in a range of conversations and collaborations with diverse partners, building on others' ideas and expressing their own clearly and persuasively.

Language

CCRA.L.4: Determine or clarify the meaning of unknown and multiple-meaning words and phrases by using context clues, analyzing meaningful word parts, and consulting general and specialized reference materials, as appropriate.

CCRA.L.5: Demonstrate understanding of figurative language, word relationships, and nuances in word meanings.

CCRA.L.6: Acquire and use accurately a range of general academic and domain-specific words and phrases sufficient for reading, writing, speaking, and listening at the college and career readiness level; demonstrate independence in gathering vocabulary knowledge when encountering an unknown term important to comprehension or expression.

Source: Adapted from NGA & CCSSO, 2010, pp. 13–14, 22, 25.

CHAPTER 14

Word Detectives

Think about your students who have the biggest vocabularies. Are these also your students who read the most? Many new words elementary students add to their vocabulary come from their reading (Baumann, 2009). Imagine, for example that your students are reading about falcons, and they come across the words *eyases*, *ornithologists*, and *stoop*. How many of your students would know what these words mean? *Eyases* is a strange word for most adults, many elementary students don't know what *ornithologists* are, and the meaning for *stoop* probably calls up an image of someone bending down or the small front porch of a house. What will your students do when they encounter these words while reading about falcons? After they read, how many of them will be able to explain that *eyases* are baby falcons, *ornithologists* are scientists who study birds, and a *stoop* is a swift dive, usually to attack prey?

Students who stop and ask themselves "I wonder what *eyases* are?" when they encounter that unfamiliar word will be able to figure it out based on the context and the picture of the baby chicks hatching out of their shells. They will figure out that ornithologists are scientists who study birds and will probably add *ornithologist* to their other words in which *-ologist* means *scientist*, such as *biologist* and *psychologist*. The description of the falcon doing a stoop and capturing its prey with its talons along with the picture will help them add another meaning of the word *stoop* to their vocabularies.

Students can figure out meanings for the words *eyases*, *ornithologists*, *stoop*, and many others using a combination of context, pictures, and, for some words, morphology. Unfortunately, rather than stopping and pondering the meaning of a new word or an old word with a new meaning while reading, many students just skip it and move on. In our experience, when students skip over words that they don't immediately recognize or connect meanings to, it leads to them having little comprehension of what they have just read. In addition, every word they skip is a missed opportunity to add a new word to their vocabulary banks.

The Common Core State Standards recognize the importance of vocabulary to aid comprehension through a focus on meaning and adding new words to students' vocabulary banks. Word Detectives is a lesson framework to help students meet the Common Core vocabulary standards. It teaches students how to use context, picture, and morphology (meaningful word parts) to figure out the meaning of new words and add new word meanings for familiar words while reading. Using the gradual release of responsibility model of instruction, the Word Detectives lesson framework combines student trios and teacher-led conversations to discuss key vocabulary.

A Sample Word Detectives Lesson

The students in this class are about to read an informational text about falcons. Mr. C. has looked through the text and chosen nine words. Many of the words will be new to students, including two with multiple meanings.

Purpose Setting and Vocabulary Building

Mr. C. begins the lesson by showing everyone the cover of the book and engaging students in a general discussion about falcons. Students share what they know about these fascinating birds. The class joker adds that the Falcons are a football team in Atlanta. Mr. C. seizes on this comment to talk about the fact that many words have more than one meaning and asks students how they know this book is about the large birds called falcons and not a football team. The students realize that the picture on the cover clearly signals that the word *falcons* in this context refers to birds. Mr. C. then sets the purpose for the lesson.

He says, "As you read about falcons, you are going to meet many words that you may not have meanings for, as well as some multimeaning words like *falcons* for which you have to figure out the meaning that fits the context. Here are nine words we are going to focus on. Before reading, we are going to pronounce the words but not talk about their meanings. We call this lesson framework Word Detectives, because you are going to be detectives and use clues from the pictures, context, and related words you know to figure out the appropriate meanings for these words."

Mr. C. writes the following words on the board and has everyone pronounce them.

ornithologist	alarmed	DDT
eyries	fledglings	plentiful
stoop	eyases	scrape

Several students suggest that they know what some words mean (*alarmed*, *scrape*, and *stoop*), but Mr. C. says that, just like *falcons*, these words might have other meanings, and they will need to use the clues to figure out what the appropriate meanings are in this context.

Mr. C. then arranges the students in trios and hands the book to one member of the trio who quickly sits in the middle and holds the book so everyone can see.

TIP

Students work together and interact more when they have just one copy of the text. Handing the book to a struggling reader gives that student an important job to do and confers status on him or her.

I Do, and You Watch

Mr. C. grabs some small sticky notes and tells the students what he is going to do: "I am going to read the first four pages and look for any of these nine words. When I find them, I will write them on these notes and place them right next to where I found them. If I find any of the words more than once, I will use another sticky note to mark all the clues to the word's meaning."

Mr. C. reads these pages aloud and puts a sticky note on the word *stoop* and two sticky notes to mark the two times the word *ornithologist* occurs. When he finishes reading these pages, he thinks aloud about what the words mean.

He says, "*Ornithologist* is an easy word to figure out! The sentence has the meaning right here when it says 'Ornithologists, or bird experts.' *Ornithologist* occurs again when the text explains how they began to solve the problem. I think ornithologists are scientists who study birds. I know that *-ologist* usually means a scientist, like with *biologist* and *psychologist*.

"*Stoop* only occurs once," he continues, "but I can figure out what it means, because the text explains that the falcon dives straight down at two hundred miles per hour and grabs its prey out of the air and that this dive is called a *stoop*. There is also an awesome picture of a falcon flying with a smaller bird in its talons. This is a new meaning of *stoop* for me."

I Do, and You Help

Mr. C. then hands out small sticky notes to all the trios.

"I need your help with the next four pages," he says. Read them, and use these sticky notes to mark any places where you see any of the nine words. Once you have all the words on these pages marked, you can help me by explaining what you think they mean."

The students read and quickly find that the text uses the word *plentiful* once and *DDT* five times. They mark them and then tell Mr. C. where to find these words.

He asks, "The book tells us that birds of prey eat mice and other animals and keep them from becoming too plentiful. Who can help me explain what *plentiful* means?"

The students explain that without birds of prey, too many mice and other little animals would roam around, so *plentiful* means there are *a lot*. Mr. C. writes the word *plenty* and helps students see the morphemic connection between these two meaning-related words.

Different students read aloud the five sentences in which *DDT* occurs and conclude that DDT is a poison sprayed on crops to kill insects. Falcons were eating the insects, and the DDT harmed the falcons' eggs. The class is glad to learn that DDT was banned, and the falcon eggs are once again producing baby falcons.

You Do It Together, and I Help

The trios work together to finish the article, hunting down the other five words and marking each occurrence with a sticky note. Mr. C. circulates and reminds them they need to not just find the words but use the clues to figure out what the words mean.

TIP

Seizing every opportunity to point out morphological relationships between words will help your students rapidly increase the size of their vocabulary banks!

The Class Debriefs

The lesson ends with each trio sharing the clues it used to figure out appropriate meanings for *alarmed, eyases, eyries, fledglings,* and *scrape.* The class has clearly enjoyed being word detectives, and Mr. C. assures students they will do more Word Detectives lessons in the future. He also reminds them that whenever they are reading, they can be word detectives: "When you read, you are always going to find words you don't have meanings for. Even when you are an adult, you will encounter new words. Before I read this, I didn't know what *eyases* and *eyries* were. You are also going to find words you know with new meanings. I didn't know that the awesome fast dive a falcon makes to catch its prey is called a *stoop* or that the nest made of rocks is called a *scrape.* You can be a word detective every time you read and use the context, pictures, and related words as clues to help you solve word meaning mysteries."

Planning and Teaching a Word Detectives Lesson

Review the text students are going to read. Select eight to ten new words for which the text has clues. Include some words for which your students know related words so they learn to analyze for morphemic connections. When possible, include a few words that you didn't know previously so students see that even adult readers need to use clues in the text to figure out meanings for words. Also, be sure to include words your students probably have meanings for that have different meanings in the text. Use the following six steps when teaching a Word Detectives lesson.

1.　Tell students the purpose of the lesson. Many students think that people just happen to know the meanings of all the words they read. When these students encounter an unfamiliar word in their reading, they skip it and move on. Breaking the skip-it habit is critical to student reading growth. Students who skip over new words miss many opportunities daily to add words to their meaning vocabularies. The vocabulary deficit grows as they progress through the grades. Students need to know that everyone encounters new word meanings while reading, and authors provide clues you can use to figure out word meanings.

2.　Display the words you have chosen, have everyone pronounce them, and write them on sticky notes. Do not let anyone suggest meanings for words. If students tell you they know what a word means, respond that they will find out if the meaning they know is the meaning in this text or if there is another meaning.

3.　Use the "I do, and you watch" and "I do, and you help" phases for several words to model for students how to use clues to help determine appropriate meanings. When possible, include in these modeling steps words with morphemic clues and words for which your students have one meaning but not the appropriate meaning.

4.　Have students work in trios ("You do it together, and I help") to complete the reading and figure out appropriate meanings for the rest of the words. Give each trio just one copy of the text and a bunch of small sticky notes. Have students mark the targeted word every time it occurs. Circulate and make sure they are not just marking words but talking about what the words mean and what clues helped them solve the word mystery.

5. Convene the class and discuss meanings for all the words the trios worked on. For each word, have students read the context in which the word occurred and explain how this context provides clues, visuals, and morphemic connections.

6. Conclude the lesson by pointing out that all readers need to be word detectives whenever they read. Review with students how they used context, pictures, and morphemic connections as clues to the meanings of words. Share with students any words you didn't have appropriate meanings for before reading the text.

Word Detectives Lessons Across the Year

Observe your students as they work together in their trios. Fade out your modeling and help as you notice they understand how to use context, pictures, and morphemic clues to figure out appropriate meanings for words. When your formative assessments indicate that most students can use clues to figure out appropriate meanings, have them complete the task independently ("You do, and I watch").

You can encourage your students to use their word detective skills while reading on their own. Designate one day a week as Word Detectives Day. (If you choose Wednesday, you can declare it Word Detectives Wednesday!) Give each student one sticky note at the beginning of independent reading time. Have students look for and mark a word they didn't know the meaning of but figured out using in-text clues. When independent reading time is over, let a few volunteers share the word they sleuthed out and what clues (context, picture, or morphology) they used to solve the mystery.

How Word Detectives Lessons Teach the Standards

The focus of the Word Detectives lesson framework is on teaching students to use all the clues in text—context, pictures, and morphology—to figure out the meanings of words that are appropriate in the text they are reading. Word Detective lessons help students meet Reading informational text standard four (RI.4) and Language anchor standards four through six (CCRA.L.4–6), all of which focus on learning word meanings from reading. As students engage in discussions about word meanings in their trios and with the whole class, they are engaging in the collaborative conversations that Speaking and Listening anchor standard one requires (CCRA.SL.1).

CCSS in a Ten Important Words Lesson

Ten Important Words is a lesson framework that teaches students how to focus on important words and ideas in an informational text. When you lead students through this lesson several times and gradually release responsibility to them, you are helping them learn the reading, writing, speaking and listening, and language skills in the following standards.

Reading
RI.2.4: Determine the meaning of words and phrases in a text relevant to a *grade 2 topic or subject area*.

RI.3–5.4: Determine the meaning of general academic and domain-specific words or phrases in a text relevant to a *grade-level topic or subject area*.

Writing
CCRA.W.2: Write informative/explanatory texts to examine and convey complex ideas and information clearly and accurately through the effective selection, organization, and analysis of content.

CCRA.W.10: Write routinely over extended time frames (time for research, reflection, and revision) and shorter time frames (a single sitting or a day or two) for a range of tasks, purposes, and audiences.

Speaking and Listening
CCRA.SL.1: Prepare for and participate effectively in a range of conversations and collaborations with diverse partners, building on others' ideas and expressing their own clearly and persuasively.

Language
CCRA.L.4: Determine or clarify the meaning of unknown and multiple-meaning words and phrases by using context clues, analyzing meaningful word parts, and consulting general and specialized reference materials, as appropriate.

Source: Adapted from NGA & CCSSO, 2010, pp. 13–14, 18, 22, 25.

CHAPTER 15

Ten Important Words

Determining the most important words in an informational text is important, because these key words convey most of the meaning and main ideas about the topic. When teachers always choose the words, students learn the word meanings, but what do they do when reading on their own? Many students, even older students, have difficulty determining what the most important words in a selection are, and thus they have difficulty determining the main ideas. Ten Important Words is a comprehension lesson framework you can use to help your students determine which words in an informational text are most important (Yopp & Yopp, 2007). When your students have chosen the most important words, they have simultaneously identified most of the major concepts or main ideas. Students also learn to write summaries with key vocabulary. Using the gradual release of responsibility model of instruction, a Ten Important Words lesson combines student trios and teacher-led collaborative conversations to discuss various aspects of the text's content.

A Sample Ten Important Words Lesson

The students in Miss A.'s class are learning about different countries and cultures and are about to read an article in a student news magazine about Ecuador. This is the first Ten Important Words lesson this class has experienced.

Purpose Setting

Miss A. begins the lesson by drawing students' attention to the world map and having students identify countries they know something about or that someone they know has been to. Miss A. then points to Ecuador on the map and asks if anyone knows anything about it. Students respond with facts they can discern from the map (like "It's in South America" and "It is next to Colombia"), but they don't have any other knowledge about Ecuador.

Miss A. says, "When we are learning about a new topic or a new place, we need to decide what the most important words are that help us learn about the topic. Often, before you read, I introduce some new words to you. But what do you do when you

TIP

This framework isn't effective with narrative texts, because these texts don't usually contain a set of content-specific key words. You can use this framework with first graders in the spring, but give them five sticky notes, and call it Five Important Words.

are reading on your own? Today, we are going to work on deciding what the most important words are on the topic of Ecuador. Once we have these important words, we will use them to write a summary of some important facts about Ecuador."

I Do, and You Watch

Miss A. assigns the students to trios and gives one person in each trio a copy of the article about Ecuador. She also gives each trio ten sticky notes.

She says, "We are going to use the sticky notes to mark the ten words you think are the most important words. We are going to choose a few together. Then, your trio will choose the others. When all the trios have chosen their ten important words, we will tally up the choices to get the class list of the most important words."

Miss A. reads the first paragraph aloud and puts a sticky note next to the word *Ecuador*.

She says, "I think the word *Ecuador* is going to be important. Who agrees with me?"

The students agree.

"The next word I think is important is *South America*," she says. "We read that Ecuador is on the continent of South America, and the map in this article only shows the continent of South America."

Again, everyone agrees, and trios place a second sticky note next to *South America*.

I Do, and You Help

Miss A. then tells students that she needs their help to choose the next important word.

She says, "Read the next paragraph, and see if you find an important word there—a word we would need to write in our summaries of what we learned about Ecuador."

The students read the next paragraph, and one trio suggests that *Quito* is an important word because it is the capital of Ecuador. Another trio suggests that *equator* is important because Ecuador is right on the equator.

Miss A. puts sticky notes on both *Quito* and *equator* and explains, "Both of those words might be two of the ten most important words, so I will mark them both. As we keep reading, we are going to come to other words that may be important. As you read, mark any word your trio thinks should be marked. You will probably run out of your ten sticky notes before you come to the end. Then, you will have to decide which of the words you have already marked are not as important to Ecuador as other words. You can then move sticky notes to those words. When you finish, your trio must decide on the ten most important words. We will then tally the words, and those that most trios chose will be the class ten."

You Do It Together, and I Help

The trios work together to choose the important words. When trios have trouble deciding, Miss A. encourages them to mark the word and continue reading.

She says, "It is really not possible to know which words are going to be in your final ten until you have read the entire article. Mark that word for now, and if you find a word that seems more important later, your trio can decide to move the sticky note."

Predictably, trios start asking for more sticky notes, but Miss A. reminds them of their purpose—to choose the ten most important words—and helps them think about what words chosen earlier might be replaced with words they are wanting more sticky notes for. Eventually, each trio settles on its ten words, although the students clearly would be happier if she just allotted them some more sticky notes!

The Class Debriefs

Once the trios have made their choices, Miss A. gathers the students and creates a class tally. She asks each trio for one of its ten words and then has the other trios indicate if they also included this word. In this lesson, the first trio shares the obvious word, *Ecuador*. All the other trios indicate they have also chosen *Ecuador*. Since there are eight trios, *Ecuador* gets eight tally marks. The second trio offers *South America*, and all the other trios also chose it; it also gets eight tally marks. The third trio offers *rain forests* as an important word. Five other trios also chose *rain forests*, and thus it gets six tally marks. Miss A. continues asking for words and tallying how many groups chose that word until she's tallied all words and votes. All eight trios chose *Ecuador*, *South America*, and *equator*. Seven trios chose *bananas* and *coffee*. *Giant tortoise*, *Galapagos Islands*, *Pacific Ocean*, *rain forests*, *mountains*, *Quito*, and *Spanish* got six votes. Since there was a tie, the class decided that there were really twelve important words! (See figure 15.1 for the final tally.)

Ecuador	‖‖‖ |||
South America	‖‖‖ |||
rain forests	‖‖‖	
bananas	‖‖‖ ||
coffee	‖‖‖ ||
giant tortoise	‖‖‖	
equator	‖‖‖ |||
Galapagos Islands	‖‖‖	
volcanoes	|||
independence	|||
Spanish	‖‖‖	
Pacific Ocean	‖‖‖	
mountains	‖‖‖	
Quito	‖‖‖	
fish	||
iguanas	||
penguins	||

Figure 15.1: Final tally for a Ten Important Words lesson on Ecuador.

TIP

The first several times you do this lesson framework, some trios will choose words they like or are interested in—such as fish *and* penguins. *As they continue to work with this lesson framework, they'll be less likely to choose unimportant words because they get a sense of which words other trios will choose and don't want to waste one of their sticky notes. Let the class tally resolve the top-ten list, and students will soon stop choosing words that are interesting but not apt to make the list.*

After the class tally, Miss A. has students write a paragraph about Ecuador using as many of the vocabulary words as they can. Students use their science and social studies notebook, which they use to record some of what they are learning during each lesson. Miss A. seizes every opportunity to have students write short pieces throughout the day. She assures them that they can include words in the tally that didn't make the top-ten list. After they write their paragraphs, they highlight the words from the class tally and count how many words they used. Miss A. lets a few volunteers read their paragraphs to the class.

Planning and Teaching a Ten Important Words Lesson

You can use the Ten Important Words lesson framework whenever students are going to read an informational text. Decide how much of the text you will use for the "I do, and you watch" modeling step of the lesson and which words you will choose. After that, it is up to students to figure out what the important words are. Use the following five steps when teaching a Ten Important Words lesson.

1. Tell students the purpose of the lesson. Informational text contains words unique to the topic but important to understanding. By identifying the most important words, you identify the most important ideas about a topic.

2. Use the "I do, and you watch" and "I do, and you help" phases to show students how you decide which words are important. Mark those words with sticky notes, and explain why they are probably going to be important.

3. Have students work in trios ("You do it together, and I help") to complete the reading and choose their ten top words. Give each trio just one copy of the text and ten sticky notes. Circulate and encourage students to mark words they think might be important, but wait until they have finished the entire piece to make their final choices. Do not give in to their pleas for more sticky notes. There may indeed be ties and thus eleven or twelve important words when you tally the votes, but limit trios to ten so students talk about why one word might be more important than another.

4. Convene the class and create the class tally. Let trios take turns sharing one of their ten words and count how many trios included that word. When you've tallied all words from each trio, determine the most important ten according to the most votes. If there is a tie, declare that there must be twelve (or eleven or thirteen) important words.

5. Have students write a paragraph including as many of the words on the class tally as they can.

Ten Important Words Lessons Across the Year

Observe your students as they work together in their trios. Fade out your modeling and help once they have the knack for choosing important words. When your formative assessments indicate that most students can pick out the important words in an informational text, have them complete the task independently ("You do, and I watch").

How Ten Important Words Lessons Teach the Standards

The focus of Ten Important Words is teaching students to determine which words in a text are the most important. Ten Important Words lessons help students meet Reading informational text standard four (RI.4) and Language anchor standard four (CCRA.L.4), which focus on learning word meanings. As students engage in discussions about words in their trios and with the whole class, they are engaging in the collaborative conversations Speaking and Listening anchor standard one (CCRA.SL.1) requires. The brief writing students do at the end of the lesson teaches students how to write summaries including key vocabulary, as Writing anchor standard two (CCRA.W.2) requires. Ten Important Words also teaches Writing anchor standard ten (CCRA.W.10), because the pieces students produce make a contribution to the routine writing the Common Core expects all students to do.

CCSS in a Be Your Own Editor Lesson

Be Your Own Editor is a lesson framework to teach students to edit their writing using proofreading skills and grade-appropriate conventions. When you lead students through this lesson several times and gradually release responsibility to them, you are helping them learn the writing and language skills in the following standards.

Writing
CCRA.W.5: Develop and strengthen writing as needed by planning, revising, editing, rewriting, or trying a new approach.

Language
CCRA.L.1: Demonstrate command of the conventions of standard English grammar and usage when writing or speaking.

CCRA.L.2: Demonstrate command of the conventions of standard English capitalization, punctuation, and spelling when writing.

Source: Adapted from NGA & CCSSO, 2010, pp. 18, 25.

CHAPTER 16

Be Your Own Editor

The Common Core State Standards call for students to write correctly along two dimensions. The first dimension consists of standard English conventions that apply to both writing and speaking; let's call it *language usage*. The second dimension consists of standard English conventions that apply only to writing; let's call it *writing mechanics*. These two dimensions cover what traditionally has been considered correct writing.

The CCSS do not expect students to always be able to meet Language anchor standard one (CCRA.L.1) on language usage and Language anchor standard two (CCRA.L.2) on writing mechanics in their first drafts, but beginning in second grade (not in kindergarten or first grade), they are required to strengthen their writing through editing with help from adults and peers (see Writing standard five [W.2.5]; NGA & CCSSO, 2010, p. 19). Editing consists of proofreading for and correcting errors of language usage or writing mechanics in one's own writing. Beginning in third grade, editing is the principal means by which students learn to meet Language anchor standards one and two (CCRA.L.1–2) for their grade (see Writing standard five [W.3–5.5]; NGA & CCSSO, 2010, p. 21). In short, editing is not merely a way of making first drafts more correct or a test of what a student already knows about correct writing, but it is also the chief means of teaching students grade-appropriate conventions of language usage and writing mechanics. This means that, as students repeatedly engage in editing, they gradually gain control of the easier conventions in their first drafts so they can concentrate on editing for more sophisticated conventions as they move up through the grades.

Because Language anchor standards one and two (CCRA.L.1–2) are best taught by having students find and fix errors in their own writing on the language and mechanics conventions they are learning, students must have something to edit! In other words, you cannot successfully teach language usage and writing mechanics to students who will not write for you or who write only a little. The expectation that students will write a lot across the school day is encapsulated in Writing standard ten (W.3.10): "Write routinely over extended time frames (time for research, reflection, and revision) and shorter time frames (a single sitting or a day or two) for a range of discipline-specific tasks, purposes, and audiences" (NGA & CCSSO, 2010, p. 21). Although Writing standard ten (W.3.10) does not apply to grades K–2, it seems unlikely that most students will be able to write routinely beginning in third grade unless they have been writing fairly regularly previously.

Because willingness to write is a prerequisite for students to benefit from editing, and many students are reluctant to take chances until they know how teachers will react to any errors they make, it is usually best for grades 2–5 teachers to have their students begin the school year by writing several first drafts that are neither edited nor marked for errors. Once students know you are not expecting error-free first drafts, they are likely to write more and consequently have the number and length of first drafts necessary to benefit from editing for the usage and mechanics conventions you are teaching.

Be Your Own Editor lessons teach students grade-appropriate conventions of standard English grammar, usage, capitalization, punctuation, and spelling by having them learn to find and correct any errors they make on those conventions in their writing. Using the gradual release of responsibility model of instruction, Be Your Own Editor combines student partners and teacher-led collaborative conversations to revise student writing.

A Sample Be Your Own Editor Lesson

This is the first lesson in editing for Mr. N.'s students. He uses the gradual release of responsibility model of instruction to teach various elements of the writing process, including editing.

Purpose Setting

Mr. N. begins his first Be Your Own Editor lesson by saying, "Today you are going to edit one of the pieces you have written. When we edit, we find and fix errors we have made. Everyone makes errors while writing. Even authors who make millions of dollars from the books they have written make errors. Even authors who win awards for being the best writers in the country or the world make errors. So, authors have to edit what they have written before they send it to their publisher. Even so, their publishing company will have a professional who does a final edit before it becomes a book. Like real authors, you will learn to find and fix some of your errors. And like real authors, when you publish a piece, you will have a final editor who corrects errors you are not ready to find and fix yourselves. In this classroom, I'll be your final editor!"

Mr. N. displays the editor's checklist (see figure 16.1) and explains that the students will learn to use it to guide their editing of what they have written. At this point in the school year, the editor's checklist has four rules (or *conventions*) on it.

> **Our Editor's Checklist**
>
> 1. Capitalize the pronoun *I*.
>
> 2. Capitalize the first word in a sentence.
>
> 3. Capitalize names of people and places.
>
> 4. Capitalize names of days of the week, months, and holidays.

Figure 16.1: Editor's checklist.

TIP

Be Your Own Editor lessons are appropriate for students in grades 2 and up. This lesson framework is most effective after students have written several pieces. When learning to edit, students can use any type of writing— personal writing, first drafts, revised drafts, and so on—as long as the writing is long enough to find and fix errors.

TIP

Starting your checklist with two or three rules all having to do with the same kind of editing convention can be appropriate for students who have had a year or two of successful editing experience. However, in second grade, editing should begin with only one rule on the checklist, and in third grade, it should begin with one or two, depending on how strong the editing instruction was for students the previous year.

Mr. N. explains each rule on the editor's checklist and asks if anyone has questions about it. He asks students to give a few examples of elements (such as names of places or dates) before going to the next rule to make sure they understand each convention they are responsible for fixing.

I Do, and You Watch

Mr. N. says, "When you edit something you've written, our editor's checklist has the only rules you need to worry about. But I expect you to learn to find and fix every one of your errors on these four rules. I am going to show you, so you will know how to do it."

Mr. N. displays a first draft he has written. He also refers to the editor's checklist. He tells students that this piece is one he might have written when he was their age. (See figure 16.2.)

I like calendars! my favorites have pictures of places like Niagara Falls in New York. Sometimes I daydream. If the picture for the month of september is the Grand canyon, i pick a date like saturday, september 27, and imagine that I will be flying out to arizona that day to see it. maybe somebody famous like Justin timberlake will be there when i am and I can take his picture!

Figure 16.2: Sample first draft.

First, he asks his students to read his piece chorally while he listens. Then, he looks at the editor's checklist and reads the first aloud. He says, "I have used the pronoun *I* several times. Let me look to make sure it's always capitalized."

He finds the two times he failed to capitalize *I* and corrects them both by writing a capital *I* in the empty space over the error. (See figure 16.3, page 150.)

Then, he proofreads his editor's checklist to confirm that he's completed the first rule and reads the second rule aloud.

He says, "I am going to look at the beginning of each of my sentences to see if I started it with a capital letter. So, I look at my first sentence. Yes, the first word there is capitalized. Now, I will look at every ending punctuation mark to make sure the next word after it is capitalized. See there? I have an exclamation mark at the end of my first sentence, but the next word is not capitalized. I need to fix that."

TIP

When you model writing, skip every other line, so it's easy to insert corrections above the errors. Starting at the beginning of the year, encourage students to do this as well. Students will follow your lead!

I like calendars! my favorites have pictures of places like Niagara Falls in New York. Sometimes I daydream. If the picture for the month of september is the Grand
                    I
canyon, i pick a date like saturday, september 27, and imagine that I will be flying out to arizona that day to see it. maybe somebody famous like Justin timberlake will
                    I
be there when i am and I can take his picture!

Figure 16.3: Sample first draft with proofreading corrections.

He also calls students' attention to the period at the end of the fourth sentence, noting that the fifth sentence doesn't start with a capital letter. Mr. N. writes the capital letter above it, and then he proofreads his editor's checklist to confirm that he's completed the second rule. (See figure 16.4.)

                M
I like calendars! my favorites have pictures of places like Niagara Falls in New York. Sometimes I daydream. If the picture for the month of september is the Grand
                    I
canyon, i pick a date like saturday, september 27, and imagine that I will be flying out to arizona that day to
            M
see it. maybe somebody famous like Justin timberlake will
                    I
be there when i am and I can take his picture!

Figure 16.4: Sample first draft with proofreading corrections.

I Do, and You Help

He then asks students to help him find and fix any errors according to the third rule. He has them read the rule chorally while he listens. Then, he waits for students to volunteer. He is patient; eventually different students notice the three errors and tell him how to correct them, and he does so. Then, he has students read the fourth rule chorally and help him find and fix the three errors for that rule. (See figure 16.5.)

> I like calendars! $\overset{M}{my}$ favorites have pictures of places
>
> like Niagara Falls in New York. Sometimes I daydream.
>
> If the picture for the month of $\overset{S}{september}$ is the Grand
>
> $\overset{C}{canyon,}$ $\overset{I}{i}$ pick a date like $\overset{S}{saturday,}$ $\overset{S}{september}$ 27, and
>
> imagine that I will be flying out to $\overset{A}{arizona}$ that day to
>
> see it. $\overset{M}{maybe}$ somebody famous like Justin $\overset{T}{timberlake}$ will
>
> be there when $\overset{I}{i}$ am and I can take his picture!

Figure 16.5: Sample first draft with proofreading corrections.

"Good. I have finished editing my draft," he explains. "With your help, I have corrected all the errors I made for the four rules on our editor's checklist."

You Do It Together, and I Help

He has the students take their pieces of writing out of their individual writing folders and select one to edit. He tells them they can choose any one they like, but that they can't choose one that is so short they won't have much to edit. If they are not sure, he has them show him the one they have picked, and he decides whether it is of sufficient length.

He partners the students in editing pairs he has chosen beforehand.

He explains, "I want you to work together with your partner to edit each of your papers for the rules on our editor's checklist. Do one rule at a time. I'll walk around and help you if you ask me to or if I notice something I want to show you."

Because students in this class had regular experience editing their own writing the previous school year, they are able to do quite well. Mr. N. notices pairs who don't seem to get along or who get along too well, and he jots a note to himself to change those partnerships before the next Be Your Own Editor lesson. He also looks to see whether anyone needs to capitalize the pronoun *I*. That is a rule he plans to remove from the editor's checklist as soon as all students have mastered it. He decides to leave it on the checklist for at least one more editing session since he notices one group correcting for it.

TIP

It is generally a good idea to pair editing partners who are fairly close in writing ability. For the handful of students who may have extreme difficulty finding their errors and correcting them, you may want to pair each of them with an average or slightly below average student.

TIP

Editing in partners for a while before editing independently is an important phase in the gradual release of responsibility model of instruction. Be on the lookout for one partner doing all the editing and the other one riding free. If you see this behavior, consider reassigning these students to other partners.

The Class Debriefs

When the time for editing in partners that day ends, Mr. N. praises the students for their hard work and has them put their edited drafts in their writing folders. He asks them if they feel they are improving in being able to find any errors they made for the rules on the editor's checklist. When a boy volunteers that he is "much better," Mr. N. suppresses a chuckle and calls for the class to give the boy a silent cheer.

Planning and Teaching a Be Your Own Editor Lesson

The two most important elements of a Be Your Own Editor lesson are the editor's checklist and the piece of writing you will edit during the "I do, and you watch" and "I do, and you help" phases. The main goal for preparing the editor's checklist at the beginning of the year is to enable students to have some success in editing their writing. It's OK if the editor's checklist is too easy at first; whenever students indicate mastery of rules in their first drafts, you are free to remove them and replace them with other rules. You can base these new rules on errors you noticed in students' first drafts.

The piece of writing you use that models one from their grade level should contain several errors, so students can see exactly how to find and fix errors when they edit their first drafts. Your piece should not be so long that it extends the lesson unduly, and ideally, its content will engage your students' interests. Obviously, you can keep a piece of writing that works well for this purpose and use it again with next year's class. Use the following three steps when teaching a Be Your Own Editor lesson.

1. At first, tell students the purpose of the lesson. It is crucial to begin each lesson with a clear explanation that every writer makes errors. There aren't any perfect writers who never make errors. So every writer needs to learn to edit what he or she has written. It is a good thing, not a bad thing, to find the errors one has made and fix them. (In second grade, in a class for students with special needs, or with a class who has not had previous success with editing, each editing session may need to begin with the purpose for the lesson.) Eventually, once students' behaviors and attitudes during editing show that they no longer need this step of the lesson, you can eliminate it.

2. For the first several Be Your Own Editor lessons, use the "I do, and you watch" and "I do, and you help" phases to model finding and correcting errors. This will get students off to a good start with editing their own writing. Be careful not to move too quickly for students who are having difficulty finding and fixing their errors. Initial success with editing is a prerequisite for success later on in the year when the conventions become more challenging.

3. Have students work in partners ("You do it together, and I help") to edit their drafts. This step will continue to be a part of each Be Your Own Editor lesson for some time, after the purpose setting and the "I do, and you watch" and "I do, and you help" phases are no longer needed. Even when only a few students need to edit in partners and the rest can do so independently ("You do it alone, and I watch"), have everyone work with partners again for at least a few sessions when you add a new rule to the editor's checklist. Again, let the students' performance during collaborative editing

time reveal when you no longer need certain phases of the gradual release of responsibility model.

Be Your Own Editor Lessons Across the Year

Gradually modify the editor's checklist. Once in a while, you may choose to eliminate a rule, but do so only when almost all students have mastered it and follow the convention correctly in their first drafts. If you are not sure whether a rule on the checklist is still necessary, design a writing prompt that will elicit several instances of that convention (for example, names of places), and then take the papers up, and mark any errors students made regarding that rule. This formative assessment will reveal whether your students still need that rule on the checklist. Then, replace old rules with new ones. You'll want to pace your adding of new rules slowly enough to ensure students continue to use the checklist with the same willingness and engagement as before.

How Be Your Own Editor Lessons Teach the Standards

Be Your Own Editor teaches Writing anchor standard five (CCRA.W.5), because the major emphasis in the lessons is helping students learn the essential editing abilities of proofreading and self-correcting their own writing for errors. Be Your Own Editor lessons also teach Language anchor standard one (CCRA.L.1). Students learn grade-appropriate conventions of standard English grammar and usage by finding and correcting any errors they make on those conventions in their writing. Similarly, students learn Language anchor standard two (CCRA.L.2) by fixing capitalization, punctuation, and spelling in their writing.

CCSS in a What's Your Opinion? Lesson

What's Your Opinion? is an instructional framework that teaches students to write first drafts of opinion pieces and use a grade-appropriate set of guidelines to revise some of them. When you lead students through this lesson several times and gradually release responsibility to them, you are helping them learn the writing skills in the following standards.

Writing

CCRA.W.1: Write arguments to support claims in an analysis of substantive topics or texts, using valid reasoning and relevant and sufficient evidence.

CCRA.W.4: Produce clear and coherent writing in which the development, organization, and style are appropriate to task, purpose, and audience.

CCRA.W.5: Develop and strengthen writing as needed by planning, revising, editing, rewriting, or trying a new approach.

CCRA.W.10: Write routinely over extended time frames (time for research, reflection, and revision) and shorter time frames (a single sitting or a day or two) for a range of tasks, purposes, and audiences.

Source: Adapted from NGA & CCSSO, 2010, p. 18.

CHAPTER 17

What's Your Opinion?

Whenever you find yourself in a conversation or near others talking in a crowd, you are likely to hear people express lots of opinions in just a few minutes. Having opinions is certainly not limited to adults. Even small children readily state whether they like a particular food and what they want for their birthday. Just listen when your students are talking among themselves during recess or playtime. You will almost certainly hear them utter different opinions about what they should do and who should perform what role. Expressing opinions seems almost as natural as communication itself.

The Common Core State Standards build on this human tendency to form and articulate personal views by having students begin to write simple opinion pieces in kindergarten and first grade. Writing anchor standard one (CCRA.W.1) seeks to improve students' ability to compose well-reasoned opinion pieces so that, increasingly, students will be able to use evidence and logic to support their judgments and conclusions in the various subjects they study as they move up through the grades.

What's Your Opinion? is an instructional framework for helping students improve their writing of opinion pieces. It requires the coordinated use of two kinds of lessons. First, several prompt-based writing lessons focus on producing an opinion piece. Second, students use guidelines to revise some of their first drafts to make them better and more complete. The instructional sequence of writing and revising opinion pieces with specific guidelines continues over time. As students' first drafts of opinion pieces improve in quality, teachers gradually make the set of guidelines longer and more sophisticated.

Using the gradual release of responsibility model of instruction, What's Your Opinion? combines student partners and teacher-led collaborative conversations to revise opinion pieces.

A Sample What's Your Opinion? Lesson

What's Your Opinion? lessons involve two parts: (1) writing opinion pieces and (2) revising opinion pieces. Mr. W. follows the five steps of a prompt-based writing lesson every time he has the students produce an opinion piece.

1. Teach or review background knowledge needed to understand the prompt.

2. Present the prompt and answer questions about it.

3. Have the students consult sources or refer to ones they have read previously to build content knowledge needed for writing their pieces.

4. Have students individually plan their writing.

5. Have students independently write in response to the prompt.

These five steps for prompt-based writing are helpful when guiding students in writing and revising a specific kind of writing—such as an opinion piece.

Writing Opinion Pieces

Mr. W. begins his prompt-based writing lesson for an opinion piece by asking his students, "Do any of you have a pet?"

A few students talk briefly about their pets. Then, he says, "Let's think of what would be some unusual pets."

Students suggest animals that would make unusual pets, and Mr. W. makes sure everyone understands the difference between common and rare pets.

Once students have an understanding of a rare pet, Mr. W. displays the prompt and reads it to his class: "'Pretend you would like to have a certain unusual pet. Write a note asking your mom or dad if you can have that pet.' I'm going to read you a book that is about a strange pet and that has notes in it."

Mr. W. reads the picturebook, *I Wanna Iguana* by Karen Kaufman Orloff and David Catrow. The story is almost exclusively a series of notes written back and forth between a boy named Alex and his mother. In the notes, Alex tries to convince his mother to let him have an iguana as a pet.

When Mr. W. finishes the book, he takes a few minutes to let the students talk about the story and whether they liked it. Then, he points to the prompt and reminds them that in a few minutes, they are going to write one note asking for an unusual pet. He shows them a couple of notes in the book again and explains notes are quite informal but usually start with *Dear* and end with the name of the person who wrote it. Mr. W. tells his students to think of a good reason why they should have the pet.

He says, "Before you start writing, I want you to decide which unusual pet you are going to choose. You can't choose an iguana. The one you choose doesn't have to be one we've talked about, but it can be. Don't tell anyone, but decide in your own mind what unusual pet you are going to ask for. I'll give you one minute to decide, and then we'll start writing."

Mr. W. uses the stopwatch on his smartphone as a timer. When the minute of think time is up, Mr. W. points to the prompt and tells them he will leave it there while they write so they can refer to it at any time. He tells them to skip every other line as they write.

TIP

When students are writing first drafts, they don't know which piece they will eventually choose to revise and edit. If they skip lines when writing, they will have room to make small revisions later by writing in the empty space above.

Revising Opinion Pieces

After students have at least three opinion pieces in their writing folders, Mr. W. prepares a lesson on revising opinion pieces. This is the first one he has taught. He uses the gradual release of responsibility model to teach various elements of the writing process, including revision.

Mr. W. begins the lesson by saying, "Today you are going to revise one of the opinion pieces you have written. When we revise, we work to make what we have written even better. We don't correct any errors we've made. Instead, we wait to do that until it is time for us to edit the piece. We aren't going to do that today."

TIP

Using the phrase even better *implies to students that their writing is pretty good to start with and revision will improve it.*

Mr. W. displays the first guideline for opinion pieces—"1. Clearly introduce the topic, book, or other text you are writing about"—and explains that the students will learn to use it to guide the revision of an opinion piece they have written.

He asks the students why they think the guideline has the number 1 by it. Some of them respond by guessing that there will be a second guideline before long, and he tells them they are right. A few try to get him to tell them what number 2 will be, but he politely refuses. Gradually, Mr. W. will add to the set of guidelines and make it longer and more sophisticated. (See figure 17.1 for the full set Mr. W. will eventually use.)

Mr. W. asks students what *topic* means. He continues to give examples and asks them for examples until he feels most of them understand what a writing topic is. He asks them to recall what they wrote about in the three opinion pieces they've done so

Our Opinion Piece Guidelines

1. Clearly introduce the topic, book, or other text you are writing about.

2. State your opinion about the topic, book, or other text.

3. Give good reasons for your opinion.

4. Use linking words to connect your opinion with your reasons.

Figure 17.1: Opinion piece guidelines.

far this year. They remember that the first piece was about the unusual pet they'd like to have, the second was about the most interesting book they have read so far this year, and the third was about the nutritious snack they like the best. They decide they wrote about a topic in their first and third pieces, and they wrote about a book in the second. He asks them what *introduce* means, and they discuss that for a few minutes. Finally, they discuss what it means to write something *clearly*.

I Do, and You Watch

Mr. W. displays a first draft (see figure 17.2, page 158) he has written on a different topic than they have written about. The first guideline for opinion pieces is still displayed as well. He tells the students that this opinion piece is one he might have written when he was their age.

First, he asks the students to read his piece chorally while he listens. Next, he reads the first guideline aloud. Then, he says, "I am going to quietly read what I have written to decide whether I have clearly introduced my topic."

> Roller coasters make me want to throw up! Pendulum rides get me so dizzy I can't walk straight when I get off. Drop towers scare me so badly I think I'm going to die. Swing rides also upset my stomach. They ought to pay me instead of me having to pay them to ride those things!

Figure 17.2: Sample first draft of an opinion piece.

After briefly looking over his opinion piece, he says, "Oh, dear, I didn't introduce my topic at all! I need to do that."

He writes a new first sentence in the space above the first line of his draft. It says, "I don't like most rides at amusement parks." (See figure 17.3.)

> I don't like most rides at amusement parks.
> Roller coasters make me want to throw up! Pendulum rides get me so dizzy I can't walk straight when I get off
> Drop towers scare me so badly I think I'm going to die. Swing rides also upset my stomach. They ought to pay me instead of me having to pay them to ride those things!

Figure 17.3: Sample first draft of an opinion piece with revisions.

I Do, and You Help

Mr. W. asks the students, "Now, I think I have introduced my topic. Can any of you tell me what you think my topic is?"

Mr. W. waits patiently with an inviting expression on his face. In time, one student asks him what an amusement park is, and he mentions the two closest to where they are. Then, a few students volunteer. When one says, "Your topic is amusement park rides," several others nod.

Mr. W. continues, "Do you think my topic is clear enough, or could it be clearer?"

At first, the students all seem satisfied, but eventually a student asks him if he liked the rides they had at the county fair earlier this month. He says, no, many of them were like the rides at an amusement park. That student suggests he add *fairs* to his first sentence, and he does so. Another student says his family went to a carnival in a nearby town last spring, which had rides. So Mr. W. adds *carnivals* to his first sentence. (See figure 17.4.)

I don't like most rides at amusement parks, fairs, and carnivals. Roller coasters make me want to throw up! Pendulum rides get me so dizzy I can't walk straight when I get off Drop towers scare me so badly I think I'm going to die. Swing rides also upset my stomach. They ought to pay me instead of me having to pay them to ride those things!

Figure 17.4: Sample first draft of an opinion piece with revisions.

Mr. W. says, "Thank you for helping me revise my opinion piece. Don't you think it's better than it was?"

You Do It Together, and I Help

Mr. W. has the students take their three opinion pieces out of their individual writing folders and select one to revise. He tells them to pick the one they like the best.

He puts the students together in revising partners. Because he has previously paired students to be editing partners and those partnerships have been working well together, he uses the same partnerships for revising.

He explains, "I want you to work together with your partner to revise each of your papers for the guideline. I'll walk around and help you if you ask me to or if I notice something I want to talk with you about. Remember that every paper can be revised for the guideline. If your paper doesn't meet the guideline, revise it so that it does. If your paper already meets the guideline, revise it so it meets the guideline in an even better way! The purpose of each guideline is to help you focus on one area of your paper and make it the best you can."

Because Mr. W. had students skip every other line on their first drafts from the beginning of the year, it is easy for them to make their small revisions. They just use a caret (^) to insert any addition or add a replacement in the empty line above what they already have written. They draw a line through anything they want to delete.

TIP

It is generally a good idea to have revising partners be fairly close in writing ability with the exception of the handful of students who may have extreme difficulty using guidelines to revise what they have written. In those few cases, you may want to pair them with an average or slightly below average student who can help them without becoming too impatient with them.

TIP

During revision, forbid students from writing a clean copy on a new sheet of paper. If they use energy to do that, they will not have enough left to address the point of revision, which is to add, replace, delete, or reorder content to make the piece clearer, more interesting, or more complete.

The Class Debriefs

Mr. W. asks the students how they feel now about the way they have introduced the topic or text their opinion piece is about. Several students agree that their revised paper does the job clearer or better. He asks them to think about what they have learned about how to introduce what they are writing about. Everyone laughs when one girl says, "Not to forget to do it!" Mr. W. responds that she is certainly right but rephrases his question to ask what students have learned about how to improve the way they have introduced their topic or text. A lively conversation ensues that he has to cut short because of time.

Planning and Teaching a What's Your Opinion? Lesson

What's Your Opinion? consists of two kinds of lessons: (1) writing opinion pieces and (2) revising opinion pieces. To teach students to revise their opinion writing, you must first have them write opinion pieces. Thus, plan prompt-based writing lessons for students to produce opinion pieces. The best prompts for elementary writers are brief, straightforward, and interesting or intriguing. Use the five prompt-based writing steps to plan the lesson: (1) teach or review background knowledge needed to understand the prompt, (2) present the prompt and answer questions about it, (3) have the students consult sources or refer to ones they have read previously to build content knowledge needed for writing their pieces, (4) have students individually plan their writing, and (5) have students independently write in response to the prompt. Opinion editorials from the local newspaper or children's books like *Dear Mrs. LaRue: Letters From Obedience School* or *Earrings!* provide good examples for students so they will understand what an opinion piece is.

After students have written several opinion pieces, move on to revision. Create guidelines that gradually increase in sophistication as students make revisions. The most important elements of the revision process are the guidelines students use to steer their revisions and the piece of writing you revise during the "I do, and you watch" and "I do, and you help" phases. The goal of the guidelines is to help student partners have some success in revising a first draft. Similarly, the piece of writing you use to model the process should clearly need revision according to the guideline being discussed. Doing so helps students see exactly how to improve their first drafts in relation to that guideline. Use the following five steps when teaching a What's Your Opinion? lesson.

1. Wait to teach revision of opinion pieces until your students have at least three first drafts of opinion pieces to choose from.

2. Tell students the purpose of the lesson. They are going to use the guidelines to revise one of their opinion pieces so it will be even better.

3. For the first several What's Your Opinion? revision lessons, and whenever you add a new guideline for opinion pieces, include the "I do, and you watch" and "I do, and you help" phases to model what you want students to do.

4. The first draft you use to model revision should be short, interesting, and on a topic or text students haven't written about. Make sure you can revise it according to the single guideline that is the day's teaching point. Expect

to include this kind of modeling for each guideline in multiple lessons until students internalize the guideline and what it means for them to do.

5. Have students work in partners ("You do it together, and I help") to revise their drafts for all the guidelines. While you should only teach students one new guideline at a time until they learn to revise successfully with it, you should eventually have them revise their first drafts for every guideline, so they do not forget or ignore the previously learned guidelines.

What's Your Opinion? Lessons Across the Year

The set of guidelines for revising opinion pieces in your classroom should always begin with a single guideline. As soon as you observe that most of your students are successful at revising their first drafts for that guideline or their first drafts no longer need revision for that guideline, add a new guideline. When most of your students are successfully revising with both guidelines, add a third. (See Mr. W.'s full set of guidelines, page 157.)

Eventually, most of your students should be able to use the current set of guidelines for opinion pieces to revise a first draft independently. However, it is always a good idea to have them work with their revising partners for a while after you add a new guideline.

How What's Your Opinion? Lessons Teach the Standards

What's Your Opinion? teaches Writing anchor standard five (CCRA.W.5), because students learn to use guidelines to revise some of their writing. The lessons teach Writing anchor standard one (CCRA.W.1), because they help students gradually learn to meet grade-appropriate guidelines in the opinion pieces they produce. The lessons help students meet Writing anchor standard ten (CCRA.W.10), because producing opinion pieces about topics and texts makes an important contribution to the routine writing the Common Core expects all students to do. Lastly, the lessons teach Writing anchor standard four (CCRA.W.4), because they help students learn to produce clear and coherent opinion pieces that meet grade-specific expectations.

CCSS in a Teach Me Lesson

Teach Me is an instructional framework that teaches students to write first drafts of informational pieces and use a grade-appropriate set of guidelines for revision. When you lead students through this lesson several times and gradually release responsibility to them, you are helping them learn the writing skills in the following standards.

Writing

CCRA.W.2: Write informative/explanatory texts to examine and convey complex ideas and information clearly and accurately through the effective selection, organization, and analysis of content.

CCRA.W.4: Produce clear and coherent writing in which the development, organization, and style are appropriate to task, purpose, and audience.

CCRA.W.5: Develop and strengthen writing as needed by planning, revising, editing, rewriting, or trying a new approach.

CCRA.W.10: Write routinely over extended time frames (time for research, reflection, and revision) and shorter time frames (a single sitting or a day or two) for a range of tasks, purposes, and audiences.

Source: Adapted from NGA & CCSSO, 2010, p. 18.

CHAPTER 18

Teach Me

The counterpart of reading to learn is writing to teach. Elementary students in the 21st century are expected to read books, articles, and websites to build their familiarity with academic topics. They are also expected to write papers that help them direct their study, organize their thinking, and reveal their knowledge and understanding. In secondary and higher education, and in most careers, being able to produce satisfactory informational writing will be essential for your students' success.

Using Teach Me, students can make steady progress toward meeting Writing anchor standard two (CCRA.W.2) by the time they leave elementary school. Teach Me helps students write clear and coherent informational pieces that meet the grade-specific expectations of the Common Core. Producing informational pieces about topics and texts can make an important contribution to the routine writing the Common Core expects all students to do.

Teach Me is an instructional framework for helping students improve their informational writing. It requires two kinds of lessons. First, students write several informational pieces from prompts. Second, students use guidelines for informational pieces to revise some of their first drafts to make them better and more complete. The instructional sequence of writing and revising informational pieces with specific guidelines continues over time. After students' first drafts of informational pieces show improvement, make the set of guidelines longer and more sophisticated.

Using the gradual release of responsibility model of instruction, Teach Me combines student partners and teacher-led collaborative conversations to write and revise informational pieces.

A Sample Teach Me Lesson

Teach Me lessons involve two parts: (1) writing informational pieces and (2) revising informational pieces. Mrs. V. follows the five steps of prompt-based writing to guide her classroom instruction for writing informational pieces.

1. Teach or review background knowledge needed to understand the prompt.

2. Present the prompt and answer questions about it.

3. Have the students consult sources or refer to ones they have read previously to build content knowledge needed for writing their pieces.

4. Have students individually plan their writing.

5. Have students independently write in response to the prompt.

These five steps for prompt-based writing are helpful when guiding students in writing and revising a specific kind of writing—such as an informational piece. To prepare her students to revise their informational writing, Mrs. V. first prepares a lesson on writing.

Writing Informational Pieces

The lesson begins with Mrs. V. helping her students review what they have been learning in their animals unit.

She says, "This week in science, we have been learning about birds. Do you remember hearing Lakesha's bird sing? Thank you again, Lakesha, for bringing him. Do you remember observing the bird feeder outside our window for five minutes and writing down what you saw and heard? Do you remember watching the YouTube video of wild geese flying a long way and then landing on a lake to sleep? Good, I'm glad you do."

Mrs. V. then displays the prompt: "Pretend you have a younger brother or sister in second grade. Write a paper for him or her to read that explains what you have learned this week about birds."

Mrs. V. says to the class, "Let's take out our science books to remember what we read about birds and what they need to live. Do you all remember? I'm glad so many of you do."

She asks students questions about how the section is organized. Of course, students volunteer various things that the authors say about birds, but she keeps bringing them back to how the section is written, that it tells them true things about birds, and doesn't give the authors' opinions about birds. "We don't know whether the authors like birds or not!" she tells them.

Mrs. V. says, "Before you start writing, I want you to take out a piece of scratch paper. Write down the three most important things you have learned this week about birds. You have two minutes. I'll walk around to help you if you need me to."

Mrs. V. uses the stopwatch on her tablet as a timer. When the two minutes are up, Mrs. V. asks students to take out their notebooks and has them read the prompt chorally. She continues to display the prompt while the students write so they can refer to it at any time and reminds them to skip every other line as they write.

She does not spell words for students while they are writing. If a student asks how to spell a word, she simply replies, "Spell it as best you can. If this is a piece you decide to edit and publish, I will help you fix the spelling then."

Revising Informational Pieces

After a few lessons on writing informational pieces, Mrs. V. prepares a lesson on revising them. Her students have had several lessons on revising their opinion pieces, so they are familiar with how revision works. This is their first lesson on revising infor-

TIP

If you spell a word for one student, you will find others wanting you to do it for them as well. Before long, you will find you are spending most of your time spelling words rather than observing students' informational writing processes. In addition, spelling words for students will slow them down while they wait for you, and they won't write as much.

mational pieces. Her students have written three different informational pieces prior to this lesson: one about birds, one about American Indian tribes, and one about the field trip they took to their county courthouse. She uses the gradual release of responsibility model to teach various elements of the writing process, including revision.

She says, "In a little while, you are going to revise one of the informational pieces you have written. You will revise it in a similar way to how you have been revising your opinion pieces. Who can tell me what we do when we revise?"

Lots of hands go up, and the student she calls on proudly says, "We make our writing even better."

Our Informational Piece Guidelines

1. Introduce the topic.

2. Give facts and details about the topic.

3. Have an ending statement or section.

4. Define a few important words if your readers might not know them.

5. Group related information together.

6. Use words like *also*, *another*, *and*, *more*, and *but* to connect related ideas together.

Figure 18.1: Informational piece guidelines.

Mrs. V. displays a set of guidelines for informational pieces and explains that the students will learn to use it to guide the revision of some of their informational pieces. Her students have already been learning to introduce their topics in their informational pieces, but she still only displays the first two guidelines. Gradually, Mrs. V. will add to the set and make it longer and more sophisticated. (See figure 18.1 for the full set Mrs. V. will use.)

Mrs. V. reminds her students that they have been revising their opinion pieces to make sure they have introduced their topic. She tells them they will also be revising their informational pieces for that guideline. Then, she has the class read the second guideline chorally while she listens. She tells students that in order to revise for this guideline, they must understand what *facts* are and how they are different than *opinions*.

She asks for volunteers to recall the topic of an opinion piece they have written this year. She follows up every response by asking the students what their opinion was in their paper. After each answer to this question, Mrs. V. turns to the class and asks if students think someone else could have had a different opinion about that topic. In each case, students agree that some people could think or feel otherwise.

Mrs. V. says, "So an opinion is something people can disagree about. You may think your opinion is right, but others think you're wrong. Your opinion might be right, but there are people who don't think so. Even a very popular opinion can turn out to be wrong."

She goes on to explain that the informational pieces they have been writing in recent weeks are not opinion pieces. She reminds them they have been trying to teach readers about a topic in their informational pieces.

She says, "When you teach people about something, it is important that you base what you write on facts. What is a fact? It is something that is real and true. How do we know whether something is a fact? If we have witnessed something ourselves, we can say it is a fact. Does the sun rise every morning? We can say this is a fact because we see the sun in the sky."

TIP

Avoid telling students that revising is how we make our writing better; they will assume you think it is not very good to start with. Use the phrase even better *instead, and your students will approach revising with a more positive outlook!*

TIP

Once you have the first three guidelines displayed for your students to use to guide their revisions, keep moving "Have an ending statement or section" down each time you add a new guideline to the set. So, it will originally be guideline three, then four, then five, and finally six.

Mrs. V. continues to have a conversation with the class about the difference between fact and opinion and writes down students' examples. She asks them for examples of facts and turns to the class each time to ask students if they agree it is a fact. In this discussion, she continues to bring them back to whether they or someone they know and trust has experienced what they are calling a fact. She contrasts these examples with opinions that the students have stated earlier in their opinion pieces until most students seem to understand that a fact is not a matter of opinion.

When some students offer examples that someone hasn't experienced—like measuring 5,280 feet in a mile—she tells them they can trust reliable sources such as encyclopedias and textbooks to confirm the fact. For each uncertain example she writes down, she helps students see how sources can help them find facts or determine whether something is a fact when they haven't experienced it themselves or know someone trustworthy who has.

I Do, and You Watch

Mrs. V. displays a first draft (see figure 18.2) she has written on a different topic than students have written about. The first two guidelines for informational pieces are still displayed as well. She tells the students that this informational piece is one she might have written when she was their age.

> Hockey is a family of sports played between two teams. Hockey players use a curved stick to try and hit the ball or the puck into the other team's goal. Some people like to watch hockey games because the players go fast.

Figure 18.2: Sample first draft of an informational piece.

First, she asks the students to read her piece chorally while she listens. Then, she asks them to read the first guideline and decide whether she has introduced her topic. One student asks her if the topic of her paper is ice hockey, and she says no. She explains that ice hockey is just one of the several kinds of hockey. No one else has any questions or suggestions to revise the first guideline. She asks them if they are satisfied that she has introduced her topic, and many of them nod.

She reads the second guideline aloud, and says, "Now, I am going to read what I have written to myself to decide whether I have given some facts about my topic."

After briefly looking over her informational piece, she says, "I do have some facts that I know are true. It is a fact that 'hockey players use a curved stick to try and hit the ball or puck into the goal.' What do you think? Is my paper based on facts?"

One student asks how she knows that "some people like to watch hockey games because the players go fast." The student says that sentence sounds like an opinion.

Mrs. V. agrees that the phrase "players go fast" is an opinion but says the phrase "some people like to watch hockey games because the players go fast" is a fact. She tells them she knows it's a fact because when she was in college, women's field hockey was her favorite sport to watch, and her main reason for liking it was how fast it goes.

"There's not much standing around in field hockey," she tells them.

She also tells them she had friends in college who said that was also one reason they liked to watch the university field hockey teams play. Most students seem to agree that what Mrs. V. has written is based on facts. She knows that the difference between fact and opinion is a difficult concept for elementary students, so she plans to continue to work on the distinction in various ways in future reading as well as writing lessons.

I Do, and You Help

Mrs. V. tells the students, "I have introduced my topic and my paper is based on facts, but I can make it even better and more complete by adding more facts. I would like you to help me revise my informational piece by adding more facts to it."

Students take turns making suggestions. After each suggestion, she asks the class to help her decide whether she should add that fact and, if so, how to word it and where to put it. She uses a caret to point to where each new fact she adds is inserted, and she writes it in the empty line above or somewhere in the margin. If there is a major disagreement among the students about whether something is a fact or not, she tries to find a source to display to help them decide. If she cannot find the information quickly, she tells them it might be a fact, but she won't include it because she isn't sure right now. When it is something minor or only one or two students seem to question something as a fact, she just tells them whether she believes it is or is not.

After the class has helped her add several facts, she says, "Thank for you helping me revise my paper by adding some facts. I think my informational piece about hockey is better now, don't you?" (See figure 18.3.)

> Hockey is a family of sports played between two teams. People have played hockey-like games for thousands of years. ∧Hockey players use a curved stick to try and hit the ball or the puck into the other team's goal. Some people like to watch hockey games because the players go fast.∧
>
> In field hockey, each side usually has eleven players on the field at a time. During a game, an ice hockey team can have up to six players on the ice.

Figure 18.3: Sample first draft of an informational piece with revisions.

TIP

Revising partners should be fairly close in writing ability with the exception of students who have extreme difficulty using guidelines to revise what they have written. You may want to pair these students with an average or slightly below average student who can help them.

You Do It Together, and I Help

Mrs. V. has the students take their three informational pieces out of their individual writing folders and select one to revise. She tells them to pick the one they like the best.

She has the students get in the same revising partnerships as when they are revising their opinion pieces.

"I want you to work together with your partner to revise each of your papers for the two informational piece guidelines," she says. "I'll walk around and help you if you ask me to or if I notice something I want to show you. You can use sources in the room or on the Internet to add facts or decide if something you included is a fact or an opinion."

Because Mrs. V. had students skip every other line on their first drafts from the beginning of the year, it is easy for them to make their small revisions. They just use a caret to insert any addition or add a replacement in the empty line above what they already have written. They draw a line through anything they want to delete.

The Class Debriefs

Mrs. V. thanks the students for working so hard today. She tells them she has enough time for two of them to share how they improved the way they introduced their topic and for two more to share how they included more or better facts and details about their topic. Several students volunteer. The sharing seems especially helpful to several students who still have questions about how best to add relevant facts and details to their paper. Mrs. V. tells them they will have an opportunity next week to revise another one of their informational pieces for the first two guidelines.

Planning and Teaching a Teach Me Lesson

Teach Me consists of two kinds of lessons: (1) writing informational pieces and (2) revising informational pieces. To teach students to revise their informational pieces, they must first write informational pieces. Thus, plan prompt-based writing lessons for students to produce informational pieces. The best informational text prompts for elementary writers are brief and easy to understand. If possible, they should also be engaging. Use the five prompt-based writing steps to plan the lesson: (1) teach or review background knowledge needed to understand the prompt, (2) present the prompt and answer questions about it, (3) have the students consult sources or refer to ones they have read previously to build content knowledge needed for writing their pieces, (4) have students individually plan their writing, and (5) have students independently write in response to the prompt. Magazines like *Time for Kids*, *Sports Illustrated for Kids*, or *National Geographic Kids*; children's books; or short, well-written sections from science or social studies textbooks provide good sources to show students what an informational piece is like and to provide them with information about the topic they are writing about.

After students have written several informational pieces, you can introduce the first new guideline for revising an informational piece and have them use it for a lesson on revising. The most important elements of the revision process are the guidelines students use and the piece of writing you revise during the "I do, and you watch" and "I do, and you help" phases of a revision lesson. The goal of the guidelines is to help student partners have some success in revising a first draft. Similarly, the piece of writing you use to model the process should clearly need revision according to the guidelines being discussed. Doing so helps students see exactly how to improve their first drafts in relation to those guidelines. Use the following five steps when teaching a Teach Me lesson.

1. Wait to teach revision of informational pieces until your students have at least three first drafts of informational pieces to choose from.

2. Tell students the purpose of the lesson. They are going to use the guidelines to revise one of their informational pieces so it will be even better.

3. For the first several Teach Me revision lessons, and whenever you add a new guideline for informational pieces, include the "I do, and you watch" and "I do, and you help" phases to model what you want students to do.

4. The first draft you use to model revision should be short, interesting, and on a topic or text students haven't written about. Make sure you can revise it according to the single guideline that is the day's teaching point.

5. Have students work in partners ("You do it together, and I help") to revise their drafts for all the guidelines. While you should only teach students one new guideline at a time until they learn to revise successfully with it, you should eventually have them revise their first drafts for every guideline, so they do not forget or ignore the previously learned guidelines.

Teach Me Lessons Across the Year

In Mrs. V.'s lesson on revising informational pieces, her students were already familiar with the first guideline from revising opinion pieces, so she started with it and a new guideline. As soon as you feel that most of your students are successful at revising their first drafts for the current guidelines or their first drafts no longer need revision for them, add a new guideline to the set. When most of your students are successfully revising with both guidelines, add a third. (See Mrs. V.'s full set of guidelines, page 165.)

Eventually, most of your students should be able to use the guidelines for informational pieces to revise a first draft independently. However, it is always a good idea to have them work with their revising partners for a while after you add a new guideline.

How Teach Me Lessons Teach the Standards

Teach Me helps students meet Writing anchor standard five (CCRA.W.5), because it provides them with instruction and guided practice in how to use guidelines to revise some of their informational pieces. It also teaches them Writing anchor standard two (CCRA.W.2), because they learn grade-appropriate guidelines for informational and explanatory writing at the application level. It helps them meet Writing anchor standard ten (CCRA.W.10), because the informational pieces about topics and texts they produce and revise make an important contribution to the routine writing the Common Core expects all students to do. Teach Me teaches Writing anchor standard four (CCRA.W.4), because it improves students' abilities to write clear and coherent informational pieces that meet grade-specific expectations.

CCSS in a Tell Me a Story Lesson

Tell Me a Story is an instructional framework that teaches students to write first drafts of narratives and use a grade-appropriate set of guidelines for revision. When you lead students through this lesson several times and gradually release responsibility to them, you are helping them learn the writing skills in the following standards.

Writing

CCRA.W.3: Write narratives to develop real or imagined experiences or events using effective technique, well-chosen details, and well-structured event sequences.

CCRA.W.4: Produce clear and coherent writing in which the development, organization, and style are appropriate to task, purpose, and audience.

CCRA.W.5: Develop and strengthen writing as needed by planning, revising, editing, rewriting, or trying a new approach.

CCRA.W.10: Write routinely over extended time frames (time for research, reflection, and revision) and shorter time frames (a single sitting or a day or two) for a range of tasks, purposes, and audiences.

Source: Adapted from NGA & CCSSO, 2010, p. 18.

CHAPTER 19

Tell Me a Story

Almost everyone enjoys a good story. Some of us prefer stories with imagined characters and events; others of us prefer stories about real people and what they did or what happened to them. Either way, there is something highly appealing about living vicariously through others for a while. Additionally, most of us like to tell stories, at least once in a while. People—especially children—who ordinarily don't have much to say will excitedly recount something that happened to them or something they saw if it was surprising, interesting, or important enough to them. It is impossible to say what the draw of stories is, but every culture seems to value them. Perhaps it is as simple as saying that, to some extent, every story imitates life. Because all of us and those we care for have a life, we intrinsically prize stories.

The CCSS ELA make use of the centrality of stories in human communication by having students from grades 1–12 "write narratives to develop real or imagined experiences or events" (CCRA.W.3; NGA & CCSSO, 2010, p. 18). What changes across the grades is the maturity of technique and structure that students are expected to employ in the narratives they write.

Tell Me a Story is an instructional framework for helping students improve their narrative writing. It teaches students to write narratives and use grade-appropriate guidelines to revise some of them. It requires two kinds of lessons. First, students write several narratives from prompts. Second, students use guidelines to revise some of their first drafts to make them better and more complete. The instructional sequence of writing and revising narratives with specific guidelines continues over time. After students' first drafts of narratives show improvement, make the set of guidelines longer and more sophisticated. Producing narratives can make an important contribution to the routine writing the Common Core expects all students to do.

Using the gradual release of responsibility model of instruction, Tell Me a Story combines student partners and teacher-led collaborative conversations to write and revise narratives.

A Sample Tell Me a Story Lesson

Tell Me a Story lessons involve two parts: (1) writing narratives and (2) revising narratives. Miss K. follows the five steps of prompt-based writing to guide her classroom instruction for writing narratives.

1. Teach or review background knowledge needed to understand the prompt.

2. Present the prompt and answer questions about it.

3. Have the students consult sources or refer to ones they have read previously to build content knowledge needed for writing their pieces.

4. Have students individually plan their writing.

5. Have students independently write in response to the prompt.

These five steps for prompt-based writing are helpful when guiding students in writing and revising a specific kind of writing—such as narratives.

To prepare her students to revise their narrative writing, Miss K. first prepares a lesson on writing. This is her third Tell Me a Story lesson for the school year, so the students are familiar with writing narratives.

Writing Narratives

Miss K. says, "For several weeks, we've been listening to and reading Greek myths. I know each of you has favorite characters from those myths. Today, I want you to choose a couple and write a new story about them."

Miss K. displays the writing prompt for the lesson: "Choose two characters from Greek mythology. They cannot come from the same myth. Write a story about what would happen if they both showed up at our school."

One student asks whether she can pick either main or minor characters from the myths. Miss K. responds that the class can use a minor character as long as students know enough characteristics to imagine what he or she might do in their school. Miss K. mentions that if they are unsure whether their two characters appear in the same myth, they should ask her before they start writing their story.

Miss K. tells the class, "If you need to, you can look back at any books on the Greek myths shelf of our classroom library or at the Greek myths you read in your reading anthology this unit. Before you start writing your story, I want you to fill out a planning sheet I have made for you."

She has two students distribute the sheet to the class. (See figure 19.1.)

The Four Ws of My Story

Who?

When?

Where?

What?

Figure 19.1: Narrative writing planning sheet.

Miss K. says, "We've talked before about how reporters often use the five Ws to tell us a news story. Today, I want you to use the first four of the five Ws to help you plan the story you are going to write about two characters from Greek mythology. I'm leaving the *why* question out for now, but in a few weeks, I'll have you add that one to your planning sheet, too."

Miss K. tells them to put all their pencils and pens down and listen to her. She explains, "I want you to decide what two characters from Greek mythology you will write about in your story and write their names down in the *Who?* box. You will also think about what you will write in the *When?* box. Your story has to take place sometime this school year, but you can choose the month, day or days, and times of day when it happens and write that. For the *Where?* box, your story has to take place on our campus, but where is up to you. The *What?* box will probably be the most difficult to fill in, because this is where you'll summarize what will happen in your story. You should take your time to plan what the main events in your story will be and then write them in the box. Do any of you have questions?"

After Miss K. answers students' questions, she says, "Now, I want you to plan your story by writing an answer to each of the four questions in the boxes. I'm going to give you some time while I walk around looking at what you have written so far and answering any questions you have."

As students begin to fill in their planning sheets, Miss K. encourages them or asks them clarifying questions. When a boy plans his story to take place entirely at night, she helps him see that he must cross through the event in his *What?* box where the principal calls 911, since principals don't stay at school all night!

The next day, Miss K. has the students take out their completed planning sheets. She tells them she wants them to write the story they planned. She continues to display the prompt while the students write, so they can refer to it at any time. She reminds them to skip every other line as they write.

After a few lessons like this one on writing narratives, Miss K. prepares a lesson on revising narratives. Her students have had several lessons on revising their opinion and informational pieces, so they are familiar with how revision works. This is their first lesson on revising narratives. Her students have written three different narratives prior to this lesson. She uses the gradual release of responsibility model to teach various elements of the writing process, including revision.

Miss K. begins this lesson by saying, "In a little while, you are going to revise one of the narratives you have written. You will revise it in a similar way to how you have been revising your opinion and informational pieces. Remember that revising is how we make our good writing even better!"

Miss K. displays the first guideline for narratives and explains that the students will learn to use it to guide their revision. Gradually, Miss K. will add to the set of guidelines and make it longer and more sophisticated. (See figure 19.2, page 174, for the full scale Miss K. will use.)

She says, "In today's revision lesson, you are going to work on how you introduce your characters and the narrator, if you have one. It really helps your readers know who your story is mainly about before they get very far into it."

TIP

Have students individually plan their writing. Narratives are better when students plan them, even when they deviate significantly from their plan in their draft. There is a discovery element in all writing, especially narrative writing, that precludes planning from being an exact practice. It is the planning, not the sticking to the plan, that helps writers!

Our Narrative Writing Guidelines

1. Introduce the narrator, one or more characters, or both.

2. Describe the setting and situation your narrator or main character is in.

3. Have a sequence of events that feels natural to your readers.

4. Have an ending that follows from what happened and what the characters experienced.

5. Use dialogue and description to tell us what happened.

6. Use dialogue or description to show how characters feel about what has happened.

7. Use concrete words and phrases and sensory details to convey what happens.

8. Use some transitional words and phrases to convey the sequence of events.

Figure 19.2: Narrative writing guidelines.

I Do, and You Watch

Miss K. displays the first draft of the start of her narrative. The guideline for narratives is still displayed as well.

She says, "I have written the beginning of a story about two characters from Greek mythology—one of which we didn't study during our unit." (See figure 19.3.)

In her first lesson, Linus told Helen, "I know you're beautiful, but you don't sing very well. Your parents hired me to teach you how to sing better, so your voice is as pretty as your face."

Helen pouted. "I don't like you. It wasn't very nice of you to tell them I couldn't carry a tune in a chariot!"

Figure 19.3: Sample first draft of a narrative.

First, Miss K. reads what she has written aloud. Then, she looks at the guideline, and says, "Now, I am going to think to myself about whether I have introduced my characters well. I don't have a narrator."

After pausing for thirty seconds or so, she says, "You can probably guess a little about my characters, Linus and Helen, from the context, but I need to tell you more about them. If I am going to introduce them properly, I need to put some more information in my draft to help you know who they are."

Miss K. adds two sentences by writing them in the margin above her first line. (See figure 19.4.)

> Linus was a famous musician and composer of songs. He also taught pupils to sing and play musical instruments.
>
> ∧ In her first lesson, Linus told Helen, "I know you're
>
> beautiful, but you don't sing very well. Your parents hired
>
> me to teach you how to sing better, so your voice is as
>
> pretty as your face."
>
> Helen pouted. "I don't like you. It wasn't very nice of you
>
> to tell them I couldn't carry a tune in a chariot!"

Figure 19.4: Sample first draft of a narrative with revisions.

I Do, and You Help

Miss K. tells the students, "I have introduced Linus. Now I want you to help me introduce Helen. How many of you remember the myth we read about her?"

Several students' hands go in the air. The first student she calls on volunteers that Helen running off with Paris was one of the causes of the Trojan War. Miss K. agrees but says that the story she is writing takes place long before that, when Helen was a young woman still living at home. Another student suggests that maybe Miss K. just needs to make sure the reader knows Helen is really beautiful. A third student points out that the narrative already tells us she is beautiful. The second student insists, it doesn't say *how* beautiful. A fourth student says Helen wasn't just another pretty face! Miss K. laughs, and so does the class.

Miss K. asks, "OK, but I need to write something that lets the readers know how special her beauty was. What can I write?"

Several students make suggestions, but one student suggests that Miss K. write that twenty-seven different Greek princes asked her to marry them. Miss K. notices several students nodding at this idea.

Miss K. adds a sentence to the end of her draft saying that Helen was considered so beautiful that twenty-seven princes asked to marry her. (See figure 19.5.)

> Linus was a famous musician and composer of songs. He also taught pupils to sing and play musical instruments.
>
> ∧In her first lesson, Linus told Helen, "I know you're beautiful, but you don't sing very well. Your parents hired me to teach you how to sing better, so your voice is as pretty as your face."
>
> Helen pouted. "I don't like you. It wasn't very nice of you to tell them I couldn't carry a tune in a chariot!"∧ Helen was considered so beautiful that twenty-seven Greek princes asked to marry her.

Figure 19.5: Sample first draft of a narrative with revisions.

Miss K. says, "Thank for you helping me revise my draft by adding information about my characters. I think the beginning of my narrative is better now, don't you?"

However, at this point, a student asks Miss K. why she didn't also include where the story was taking place—their school. Miss K. explains that that will be the second revision guideline for narratives!

You Do It Together, and I Help

Miss K. has students take their three narratives out of their individual writing folders and select one to revise. She tells them to pick the one they like the best.

She has the students get together in the same revising partnerships she puts them in whenever they revise and explains what they are going to do.

She says, "Work together with your partner to revise your papers for the guideline. I'll walk around and help you if you ask me to or if I see something I want to point out. If you need to check on a character before adding information about him or her to your draft, you can look back at books on the Greek myths shelf or your reading anthology."

Because Miss K. had students skip every other line on their first drafts from the beginning of the year, it is easy for them to make their small revisions. They just use a caret (^) to insert any addition or add a replacement in the empty line above what they already have written. They draw a line through anything they want to delete.

The Class Debriefs

When Miss K. tells students the time for revision that day is up, they put their revised pieces in their writing folders. She asks them how they feel about revising without copying their papers over. Some students respond that they would like to copy their papers over so they look better. She explains that if she has them edit and publish the piece they worked on today, they will copy their revised and edited piece over as the last step.

A boy tells the class that he is glad he isn't allowed to copy it over before revising or editing, because "It seems like I always skip a line or make a new spelling error when I copy my paper. I have trouble keeping my mind on what I'm doing; it's so boring."

Miss K. agrees that copying can be difficult.

She says, "When it comes time for you to publish one of your stories, I'll have you copy over your revised and edited versions all at the same time, so I can walk around and help you do it well."

Planning and Teaching a Tell Me a Story Lesson

Tell Me a Story consists of two kinds of lessons: (1) writing narratives and (2) revising narratives. To teach students to revise their narratives, they must first write some narratives. Thus, plan prompt-based writing lessons for students to produce narratives. The best narrative prompts for elementary writers are brief, unintimidating, and interesting. Use the five prompt-based writing steps to plan the lesson: (1) teach or review background knowledge needed to understand the prompt, (2) present the prompt and answer questions about it, (3) have the students consult sources or refer to ones they have read previously to build content knowledge needed for writing their pieces, (4) have students individually plan their writing, and (5) have students independently write in response to the prompt. Miss K.'s lesson had students write a story that used characters from myths they had been listening to and reading in a unit. Such prompts often help students when they are first writing a narrative, because they don't have to create the characters. If you choose to do something similar, it is usually more successful if you have several stories your students are familiar with to select from as the source of their characters. That way, different stories can have different characters. Stories from your literature or reading anthology or that you have read aloud make good resources for characters as long as your class enjoyed the stories.

After students have written several narratives, have students select one of them to revise. The most important elements of the revision process are the guidelines students use and the piece of writing you revise during the "I do, and you watch" and "I do, and you help" phases. In addition, the class discussion during the "I do, and you help" phase can be invaluable in helping each student think like a writer. The goal of the guidelines is to help student partners have some success in revising a first draft. Similarly, the narrative you use to model the process should clearly need revision according to the guidelines being discussed. Doing so helps students see exactly how to improve their first drafts in relation to those guidelines. Use the following five steps when teaching a Tell Me a Story lesson.

1. Wait to teach revision of narratives until your students have at least three narrative first drafts to choose from.

2. Tell students the purpose of the lesson. They are going to use the guidelines to revise one of their narratives to make it even better.

3. For the first several Tell Me a Story revision lessons, and whenever you add a new guideline for narratives, include the "I do, and you watch" and "I do, and you help" procedures to model what you want students to do.

4. The first draft you use to model revision should be brief and interesting. Make sure you can revise it according to the single guideline that is the day's teaching point.

5. Have students work in partners ("You do it together, and I help") to revise their drafts for all the guidelines. While you should only teach students one new guideline at a time until they learn to revise successfully with it, you should eventually have them revise their first drafts for every guideline, so they do not forget or ignore the previously learned guidelines.

Tell Me a Story Lessons Across the Year

As soon as you observe that most of your students are successful at revising their first drafts for the current set of guidelines or their drafts no longer need revision for them, add a new guideline. (See Miss K.'s full set of guidelines, page 174.)

Eventually, most of your students should be able to use the current guidelines for narratives to revise a first draft independently. However, it is always a good idea to have them work with their revising partners for a while after you add a new guideline.

How Tell Me a Story Lessons Teach the Standards

Tell Me a Story teaches students Writing anchor standard five (CCRA.W.5), because it helps them learn to use guidelines to revise some of their writing. The lessons teach Writing anchor standard three (CCRA.W.3), because they help students gradually learn to meet grade-appropriate guidelines in the narratives they write. The lessons help students meet Writing anchor standard ten (CCRA.W.10), because writing narratives makes an important contribution to the routine writing the Common Core expects all students to engage in. The lessons teach Writing anchor standard four (CCRA.W.4), because they help students learn to produce clear and coherent narratives that meet grade-appropriate criteria.

CCSS in a You're the Expert! Lesson

You're the Expert! is a lesson framework that teaches students to do and present research. When you lead students through this lesson several times and gradually release responsibility to them, you are helping them learn the reading, writing, speaking and listening, and language skills in the following standards.

Reading
CCRA.R.7: Integrate and evaluate content presented in diverse media and formats, including visually and quantitatively, as well as in words.
RI.4.9: Integrate information from two texts on the same topic in order to write or speak about the subject knowledgeably.
RI.5.9: Integrate information from several texts on the same topic in order to write or speak about the subject knowledgeably.

Writing
CCRA.W.7: Conduct short as well as more sustained research projects based on focused questions, demonstrating understanding of the subject under investigation.
CCRA.W.8: Gather relevant information from multiple print and digital sources, assess the credibility and accuracy of each source, and integrate the information while avoiding plagiarism.

CCRA.W.9: Draw evidence from literary or informational texts to support analysis, reflection, and research.

Speaking and Listening
CCRA.SL.1: Prepare for and participate effectively in a range of conversations and collaborations with diverse partners, building on others' ideas and expressing their own clearly and persuasively.
CCRA.SL.4: Present information, findings, and supporting evidence such that listeners can follow the line of reasoning and the organization, development, and style are appropriate to task, purpose, and audience.
CCRA.SL.5: Make strategic use of digital media and visual displays of data to express information and enhance understanding of presentations.
CCRA.SL.6: Adapt speech to a variety of contexts and communicative tasks, demonstrating command of formal English when indicated or appropriate.

Language
CCRA.L.1: Demonstrate command of the conventions of standard English and usage when writing or speaking.

Source: Adapted from NGA & CCSSO, 2010, pp. 10, 14, 18, 22, 25.

CHAPTER 20

You're the Expert!

What are you an expert in? You are probably an expert in teaching elementary students, and you may be an expert in a different topic, such as baseball, London, or U.S. national parks. An expert is someone who has a huge amount of knowledge and expertise in one small area. Nobody is born an expert. Rather, we become interested in an area and take every opportunity to learn about it. *Research* is a daunting concept for many students—and many teachers. But research is simply choosing an area of interest and finding out all you can about it. As you research a topic, you become an expert on that topic. You're the Expert! lessons teach elementary students how to do research by helping them become experts on one small piece of a larger topic. Students will learn to formulate questions, collect and summarize information from sources, take notes, and provide a list of sources. You're the Expert! lessons culminate in students creating presentations in which they use formal English to share important information on their topics. The presentations include digital media and visual displays.

Using the gradual release of responsibility model of instruction, You're the Expert! combines student groups and teacher-led collaborative conversations to do and present research.

A Sample You're the Expert! Lesson

It is almost time for the Olympics, and the gym teacher is organizing a series of Olympic events at school. Students are excited about these upcoming events, so Mr. J. decides to capitalize on their interest and center their first research endeavor on the Olympics. In the week before the beginning of the research lessons, Mr. J. has built some general knowledge about the Olympics by using Olympics-related books and magazines during his daily read-aloud.

Purpose Setting

Mr. J. begins the first research lesson by displaying some of the pieces he shared with students during his read-aloud last week and asking students to do a quick write in which they have one minute to write down as many facts as they can about the Olympics. Everyone knows a lot, and when the timer signals the end of the minute, students eagerly raise their hands to share what they know. When they have exhausted their communal knowledge about the Olympics, Mr. J. explains what they are going to do next.

He says, "You all know a lot about the Olympics, but because it is such a huge topic, there is so much more to know. More than twenty sports are involved in the Olympics, and some of these—such as track and field and gymnastics—have many separate events. Today, we are going to list the sports and events you know are part of the Olympics, and then each of you is going to make a first, second, and third choice of a sport or event you want to become an expert on. I will put you together in Olympic teams and give each team one of your three choices. Your team members will research that sport or event—finding out everything you can about it. Your team members will become the experts on that event, and in a few weeks, you will present everything you have learned to the class—and maybe to another class or two in the school."

The students are excited about becoming experts on some part of the Olympics, and they brainstorm this list of sports. For the sports with lots of different events, Mr. J. helps them list events they are most familiar with. They come up with the following list.

- Basketball
- Soccer
- Tennis
- Gymnastics
- Floor exercises
- Vaults
- Bars
- Track and field
- Races
- Hurdles
- Jumps
- Throws
- Hockey
- Swimming
- Skiing
- Skating
- Snowboarding

TIP

The K-W-L teaching model (Ogle, 1986) helps students access their prior knowledge and set purposes for learning. First, they brainstorm what they know, *then they list questions they* want *to find answers to, and finally they list answers and additional facts they* learned *after reading.*

This class is used to creating K-W-L charts to focus their learning on particular topics. Mr. J. reminds students that the *W* stands for what they *want to know* and asks them to come up with questions that apply to most of the sports they have listed. He records these in the first column of a chart and then labels the other two columns *Notes* and *Sources* (see figure 20.1, page 183). He explains that they will record answers they find in the Notes column and list where they found the information in the Sources column.

Finally, he says, "As you know, when we do a K-W-L, we often find interesting facts that don't directly answer any of our questions. The *L* includes answers to some of our questions and also other interesting things we learned."

He adds some rows at the bottom of the chart for these other interesting facts.

This introductory class session ends with students handing in a sheet listing their first, second, and third choices and a reason for that choice. Mr. J. promises that everyone will get one of his or her choices—but not necessarily his or her first choice.

Topic and Questions	Notes	Sources
When and where did this sport begin?		
In what countries is this sport most popular?		
How is the sport played?		
How do you win?		
What special equipment does this sport require?		
Is it played indoors or outdoors?		
Is it a team or individual competition?		
When did this sport become part of the Olympics?		
Is it in the summer or winter Olympics?		
Which countries have won the most medals in this sport?		
Who are some famous Olympians for this sport?		
Other fascinating facts		
Other fascinating facts		
Other fascinating facts		

Figure 20.1: You're the Expert! chart on the Olympics.

After school, Mr. J. assigns students to teams. Most of the teams have three members, but in order to give everyone one of his or her choices and include different levels of students on each team, he forms two teams with four members. Since many students did not choose the track event of racing, and Mr. J. ran track in college, he decides he will make track his event.

Over the next several days, Mr. J. and the librarian work together in the library to find ways of demonstrating how to locate information, take notes and document sources, and create a PowerPoint presentation. Mr. J. uses the gradual release of responsibility model for this lesson.

I Do, and You Watch

Students are excited to become experts on their sport and event. They are also intrigued to know that their teacher was quite the track star in college. When they get to the library, they discover that the librarian has amassed a wide variety of print and digital resources to get them started in locating information. Mr. J. shares snippets from some of the books and magazine articles about the various running events in the Olympics. Next, he uses a safe search engine, KidRex, to find Internet sources related to the key words *running* and *Olympics*. He makes brief stops at several of the sites and bookmarks the ones he wants to return to.

For the rest of the period, the students work in their teams locating print resources and bookmarking sites they think will yield lots of information. Mr. J. and the librarian help them use book indexes and tables of contents to decide which sources are most relevant to their sport and to navigate through the digital resources.

I Do, and You Help

When the class returns to the library the next day to take notes and document sources, students are eager to find information on their sports in the sources they have located. Mr. J. tells them that before they get into their resources, he wants to show them how he will begin to research his event: running. He asks the teams to gather together, and he gives each team one sheet with the list of questions on it.

He writes *running* in the upper-left box on his sheet, and the scribes write their sport and event on their sheets. Together, they read the questions, and he tells them that they are going to help him decide if what they read in his sources answers any of the questions, and if they notice other interesting facts he should record on his sheet. He picks up a book he chose the day before titled *The 100 Greatest Track and Field Battles of the Twentieth Century*.

He says, "In this book, the author, Jeff Hollobaugh, counts down what he considers to be the greatest battles in Olympic track-and-field competitions over one hundred years. I can't read it all now—I probably will over the weekend—but the author counts down from number 100 to number 1. I am going to start at the back because I want to know what he considers to be the number 1 battle."

Mr. J. turns to the back of the book and reads the chapter title: "No. 1—Olympic Men's 10,000, Tokyo 1964: Mills Shocks the World."

He says, "I know this is a running event, because the 10,000-meter race is a long-distance run."

He then reads aloud the short description of how a Sioux Indian and U.S. Marine, Billy Mills, ran the 10,000-meter race—slightly more than six miles—in just over twenty-eight minutes, beating out the favorites by a fraction of a second.

The students listen in amazement. Mr. J. draws their attention to the list of questions and asks if this answers any of the questions on his chart. The students immediately see that Billy Mills was one of the great Olympic runners, and Mr. J. records his notes

TIP

Research is the perfect opportunity to partner with your librarian. Give your librarian lots of advanced warning so he or she can accumulate as many resources as possible. Schedule the research classes in the library where you will have the most resources as well as digital technology such as digital cameras, SMART Boards, and multiple computers.

TIP

Hand the sheet to the most fluent writer on each team, and appoint that person the team scribe.

and source next to that question, using a digital camera so that students can see how he takes notes. Working backward, he skips any nonrunning events.

Next, he goes to one of the sites he had bookmarked at the library, reads about the history of the Olympic Games, and learns that running was one of the original events in the ancient Greek games and that the original Olympians ran naked. The students tell him that this fact answers the question of when running became part of the Olympics. They insist that he include the "naked part" under other interesting facts! (See figure 20.2 for Mr. J.'s chart.)

Running	Notes	Sources
When and where did this sport begin?		
In what countries is this sport most popular?		
How is the sport played?		
How do you win?		
What special equipment does this sport require?		
Is it played indoors or outdoors?		
Is it a team or individual competition?		
When did this sport become part of the Olympics?	Running was one of the original events when the Olympics started in Greece in 776 BC.	Information from the official Olympic Games website (www.olympic.org) on the ancient Olympic Games
Is it in the summer or winter Olympics?		
Which countries have won the most medals in this sport?		

Figure 20.2: Sample You're the Expert! chart on the Olympics filled in.

Continued →

Running	Notes	Sources
Who are some famous Olympians for this sport?	Billy Mills, Sioux Indian and US marine, won gold by running slightly more than six miles (the 10,000-meter race) in just over twenty-eight minutes. Mary Decker, United States, took gold in the 3,000- and 1,500-meter races away from the favored Soviets in 1983.	Jeff Hollobaugh The 100 Greatest Track and Field Battles of the Twentieth Century
Other fascinating facts	Ancient Olympians ran naked!	Information from the official Olympic Games website (www.olympic.org) on the ancient Olympic Games
Other fascinating facts		
Other fascinating facts		

You Do It Together, and I Help

Having watched and helped their teacher take notes and document sources, the teams are eager to dig into the sources they selected yesterday to prepare their presentations. For the rest of the period, teams use their sources to work on becoming experts on their sports and events. Mr. J. and the librarian circulate, helping the students locate information within their sources and reminding them that they can't start at the beginning and read the whole text. (Several students declare that they are going to check out books over the weekend and, like their teacher, read them cover to cover!)

For the next four days, the class begins with Mr. J. modeling finding information in both print and digital sources and engaging students in helping him decide what questions are answered, what other interesting facts to include, and how to document sources. Students then work together in their teams. They need a lot of help winnowing down the information to brief notes, and Mr. J. is really glad the librarian is there, since this endeavor almost requires two coaches!

After several days of research and having answered all but one of his questions and adding five other fascinating facts to his chart, Mr. J. declares he is now expert enough to prepare his presentation on running. The students watch and make suggestions as he creates a PowerPoint presentation, which includes the facts he learned augmented by visuals and one short videoclip. He includes a notes section for each slide, which is the script for what he will say as each slide is displayed. The final slide of his presentation lists all the sources.

For the next several days, Mr. J. and the librarian coach the teams as they put together their presentations.

The Class Debriefs

Over the next several days, the teams share their presentations with their class, and the class members ask each other questions. They then revise their presentations based on the questions from their classmates and share these presentations with several other classes in the school.

Planning and Teaching a You're the Expert! Lesson

For the first venture into research, choose a broad topic that your students can get excited about. If a zoo trip is in your future, your students would probably love becoming experts on some of the zoo animals. Plan a virtual trip around the world—or around the United States or your state—and have students become experts in each of the areas you will visit. Learning how to do research requires lots of time and many different reading, writing, speaking and listening, and language abilities. Once your students understand the process, you can help them use their skills to investigate topics in your curriculum in which they may be less interested.

Use read-alouds and other resources to build some prior knowledge on the broad topic before you begin the actual research. This will pique everyone's interest and give your students a basis for making their first, second, and third choices for their expert topics. This general knowledge will also enable your class to formulate good questions. Knowing what you are looking for is essential to successful research. Use the following nine steps when teaching a You're the Expert! lesson.

1. Set the purpose for the lesson. Talk with students about experts they know and what they are currently experts in. Help them understand that you become an expert by finding out a lot about the topic and that you don't become an expert overnight. Help them view research as one way you become an expert.

2. Remind students of what you have read, shared, and experienced with them to build general knowledge of the topic. Give students one minute to write

down everything they know about the broad topic. Have students share what they wrote during this quick write and establish the status of class knowledge on the topic.

3. Have your class brainstorm a list of subtopics in which students would like to become experts. Have students give you their first, second, and third choices and their reasons for these choices.

4. Form teams of three or four students, making sure to give each student one of his or her three choices. Each team should include a range of reading and writing abilities and (hopefully) students who like each other.

5. Have the class brainstorm a list of questions that apply to most of their expert topics. Create a sheet with these questions, a column for notes, and a column for sources. Include extra rows for other interesting facts.

6. Choose an expert topic for yourself that your students have not chosen. Model for your students how you locate print and digital sources to begin your research ("I do, and you watch"). Use a safe search engine, and bookmark likely digital sources. Have teams work together to locate sources, and provide guidance as the teams assemble sources.

7. Demonstrate how you locate information within sources ("I do, and you watch"). Next, demonstrate how you cite sources ("I do, and you watch"). Let students help you decide which questions you've answered, which other interesting facts to include, and what to write in the notes ("I do, and you help").

8. Have teams work together to take notes and cite sources. Help them locate appropriate sections of resources for their topics and decide which questions are answered and which interesting facts to include. Help them keep notes brief. Let students watch and help you create a presentation, including audiovisuals, graphics, notes with a script, and sources. Help them create their presentations ("You do it together, and I help").

9. Let each expert team share its presentation with the class. Have class members ask questions, and help teams revise their presentations based on these questions. Have teams share their revised presentations with other classes or with parents.

You're the Expert! Lessons Across the Year

Research is an important but complex and sophisticated skill. Continue to teach You're the Expert! lessons across the year and provide students the modeling and support they need to develop their burgeoning inquiry skills. Depending on the age and ability of your students, you may want them to pursue an individual research project late in the year.

How You're the Expert! Lessons Teach the Standards

You're the Expert! lessons teach students how to do and present research and move students toward achieving many different standards including Reading anchor standard seven (CCRA.R.7) and Reading informational text standard nine (RI.9), which specify that students learn to integrate information from a wide variety of print and digital sources. Writing anchor standards seven, eight, and nine (CCRA.W.7–9) focus on students gathering information and conducting research projects. You're the Expert! lessons culminate in students creating presentations in which they use formal English to share important information on their topics. The presentations include digital media and visual displays. These presentations help student meet Speaking and Listening anchor standards one, four, five, and six (CCRA.SL.1, 4–6) and Language anchor standard one (CCRA.L.1).

References and Resources

Baumann, J. F. (2009). Vocabulary and reading comprehension. In S. E. Israel & G. G. Duffy (Eds.), *Handbook of research on reading comprehension* (pp. 323–346). New York: Routledge.

Browne, A. (1998). *Voices in the park*. New York: DK.

Coleman, D., & Pimental, S. (2012). *Revised publisher's criteria for the Common Core State Standards in English language arts and literacy, grades 3–12*. Accessed at www.corestandards .org/assets/Publishers_Criteria_for_3-12.pdf on May 27, 2014.

Cunningham, J. W., & Moore, D. W. (1986). The confused world of main idea. In J. F. Baumann (Ed.), *Teaching main idea comprehension* (pp. 1–17). Newark, DE: International Reading Association.

Fisher, D., Frey, N., & Nelson, J. (2012). Literacy achievement through sustained professional development. *The Reading Teacher, 65*(8), 551–563.

Herber, H. L. (1978). *Teaching reading in content areas* (2nd ed.). Englewood Cliffs, NJ: Prentice-Hall.

Hollobaugh, J. (2012). *The 100 greatest track and field battles of the twentieth century*. Dexter, MI: Michtrack Books.

National Assessment Governing Board. (2008). *Reading framework for the 2009 National Assessment of Educational Progress*. Washington, DC: U.S. Government Printing Office.

National Governors Association Center for Best Practices & Council of Chief State School Officers. (2010). *Common Core State Standards for English language arts and literacy in history/social studies, science, and technical subjects*. Washington, DC: Authors. Accessed at www.corestandards.org/assets/CCSSI_ELA%20Standards.pdf on February 21, 2014.

Ogle, D. M. (1986). K-W-L: A teaching model that develops active reading of expository text. *The Reading Teacher, 39*(6), 564–570.

Pearson, P. D., & Gallagher, M. C. (1983). The instruction of reading comprehension. *Contemporary Educational Psychology, 8*(3), 317–344.

Wilhelm, J. D. (2001). *Improving reading comprehension with think-aloud strategies*. Jefferson City, MO: Scholastic Professional Books.

Yopp, R. H., & Yopp, H. K. (2004). Preview-predict-confirm: Thinking about the language and content of informational text. *The Reading Teacher, 58*(1), 79–83.

Yopp, R. H., & Yopp, H. K. (2007). Ten important words plus: A strategy for building word knowledge. *The Reading Teacher, 61*(2), 157–160.

Index

A

anchor standards, 3
anticipation-guide strategy, 11

B

Be Your Own Editor
    CCSS for, 9, 146, 147–148, 153
    checklist, 148
    class debriefs, 152
    first drafts, 149, 150, 151
    "I do, and you help," 151
    "I do, and you watch," 149–150
    lesson purpose, 148–149
    planning and teaching, 152–153
    sample lesson, 148–152
    "You do it together, and I help," 151

C

CCSS ELA (Common Core State Standards for
        English language arts)
    goals of, 4–7
    lesson frameworks and, 9
    number of standards for K–5, 1–3
    terminology for, 3
choral reading, 123, 124, 129
Compare and Contrast
    CCSS for, 9, 72, 83
    class debriefs, 77, 80–81
    "I do, and you help," 78
    "I do, and you watch," 77–78
    lesson purpose, 73–77
    planning and teaching, 81–82
    sample lessons, 73–81
    "You do it together, and I help," 78–80

D

data charts, 73, 81
domains, 3
dot notation, 3
double bubbles (Venn diagrams), 73, 74, 75, 79

E

echo reading, 122, 123, 129, 131

F

Find It or Figure It Out
    CCSS for, 9, 20, 25
    class debriefs, 24
    "I do, and you help," 23
    "I do, and you watch," 23
    lesson purpose and vocabulary building, 22–23
    planning and teaching, 24–25
    sample lesson, 21–24
    "You do it together, and I help," 24

G

Gist
    CCSS for, 9, 32, 33, 39
    class debriefs, 38
    "I do, and you help," 36–38
    "I do, and you watch," 34–36
    lesson purpose, 33, 34
    planning and teaching, 38–39
    sample lesson, 33–38
grade levels and grade bands, 3
grade-specific standards, 3
gradual release of responsibility model of instruction, 7
Guess Yes or No
    CCSS for, 9, 10, 18

class debriefs, 16–17

"I do, and you help," 15

"I do, and you watch," 14–15

lesson purpose and vocabulary building, 12–14

planning and teaching, 17–18

sample lesson, 11–17

"You do it together, and I help," 15–16

H

Herber, H., 11

K

K-W-L charts, 182

L

lesson frameworks, CCSS and, 9

See also name of framework.

M

Main Idea Tree

CCSS for, 9, 52, 61

class debriefs, 58, 59

"I do, and you help," 55–56, 59

"I do, and you watch," 55, 58

lesson purpose, 53, 54, 58

planning and teaching, 59–61

sample lessons, 53–59

"You do it together, and I help," 56–57, 59

N

National Assessment of Educational Progress (NAEP), 5

Nation's Report Card, 5

P

Plays Aloud

CCSS for, 9, 128, 133

lesson purpose, 129

"Little Red Hen, The," 130–132

planning and teaching, 132–133

sample lesson, 129–132

Poetry Aloud

CCSS for, 9, 120, 127

class debriefs, 124

"Five Little Monkeys," 123

"Itsy Bitsy Spider, The," 122–123

lesson purpose, 121

planning and teaching, 124–127

sample lesson, 122–124

"Squirrel, The," 123–124

Point of View

CCSS for, 9, 104, 105, 117–118

class debriefs, 111–112, 115

"I do, and you help," 109, 113

"I do, and you watch," 107–109, 112–113

lesson purpose, 105, 106–107, 112

planning and teaching, 115–117

sample lessons, 106–115

"You do it together, and I help," 111, 114–115

Preview-Predict-Confirm

CCSS for, 9, 96, 103

class debriefs, 101–102

"I do, and you help," 99

"I do, and you watch," 98–99

lesson purpose, 97–98

planning and teaching, 102–103

sample lesson, 97–102

"You do it together, and I help," 99–101

Q

Question It

CCSS for, 9, 26, 27, 31

class debriefs, 29–30

"I do, and you help," 28–29

"I do, and you watch," 28

lesson purpose and vocabulary building, 27, 28

planning and teaching, 30–31

sample lesson, 28–30

"You do it together, and I help," 29

R

reading

choral, 123, 124, 129

echo, 122, 123, 129, 131

independent, 6–7

reading comprehension

defined, 5

goals of, 4–5

independent, 6–7

Reading standards, goals of, 4–5

rhymes, 125, 126

S

Sequence / Cause and Effect

CCSS for, 9, 62, 63, 71

class debriefs, 67, 69

"I do, and you help," 66, 68

"I do, and you watch," 65–66, 68

lesson purpose, 63, 64–65, 67–68

planning and teaching, 69–70

sample lessons, 63–69

"You do it together, and I help," 67, 68

step maps, 67–69

story maps, 42, 43, 44, 45

strands, 3

T

Teach Me

    CCSS for, 9, 162, 169

    class debriefs, 168

    "I do, and you help," 167

    "I do, and you watch," 166–167

    informational pieces, writing and revising, 164–166

    lesson purpose, 163

    planning and teaching, 168–169

    sample lesson, 163–168

    "You do it together, and I help," 168

Tell Me a Story

    CCSS for, 9, 170, 171, 178

    class debriefs, 177

    "I do, and you help," 175–176

    "I do, and you watch," 174–175

    lesson purpose, 171

    narratives, writing and revising, 172–174

    planning and teaching, 177–178

    sample lesson, 172–177

    "You do it together, and I help," 176–177

Ten Important Words

    CCSS for, 9, 140, 145

    class debriefs, 143–144

    "I do, and you help," 142

    "I do, and you watch," 142

    lesson purpose, 141–142

    planning and teaching, 144

    sample lesson, 141–144

    "You do it together, and I help," 142–143

Text Features Scavenger Hunt

    CCSS for, 9, 84, 85, 93–94

    class debriefs, 91–92

    "I do, and you help," 90

    "I do, and you watch," 87–90

    lesson purpose and vocabulary building, 85, 86

    planning and teaching, 93

    sample lesson, 86–92

    "You do it together, and I help," 90–91

Themes, Morals, and Lessons Learned

    CCSS for, 9, 40, 41, 50

    class debriefs, 45, 47–48

    "I do, and you help," 44, 46–47

    "I do, and you watch," 43–44, 46

    lesson purpose, 41, 43, 46

    list of common themes, 42

    planning and teaching, 48–50

    sample lessons, 42–48

    "You do it together, and I help," 44, 47

timelines, 63–67

V

Venn diagrams (double bubbles), 73, 74, 75, 79

W

What's Your Opinion?

    CCSS for, 9, 154, 155, 161

    class debriefs, 160

    "I do, and you help," 158–159

    "I do, and you watch," 157–158

    lesson purpose, 155

    planning and teaching, 160–161

    sample lesson, 156–160

    writing and revising opinion pieces, 156–157

    "You do it together, and I help," 159

Word Detectives

    CCSS for, 9, 134, 139

    class debriefs, 138

    "I do, and you help," 137

    "I do, and you watch," 137

    lesson purpose and vocabulary building, 135–136

    planning and teaching, 138–139

    sample lesson, 136–138

    "You do it together, and I help," 137–138

writing

    defined, 6

    goals of, 5–6

    independent, 6–7

Writing standards, goals of, 5–6

Y

You're the Expert!

    CCSS for, 9, 180, 188–189

    class debriefs, 187

    "I do, and you help," 184–186

    "I do, and you watch," 184

    lesson purpose, 181, 182–184

    planning and teaching, 187–188

    sample lesson, 181–187

    "You do it together, and I help," 186–187

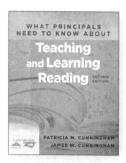

What Principals Need to Know About Teaching and Learning Reading, Second Edition
Patricia M. Cunningham and James W. Cunningham
Principals will discover strategies for improving reading programs using the foundation established by the six truths of reading instruction. Explore comprehensive techniques, troubleshoot problems your teachers may face, and gain valuable approaches to topics such as reading comprehension, vocabulary and literacy, and phonics and fluency.
BKF563

Common Core English Language Arts in a PLC at Work™ Series
Douglas Fisher and Nancy Frey
These teacher guides illustrate how to sustain successful implementation of the Common Core State Standards for English language arts in K–12 instruction, curriculum, assessment, and intervention practices within the powerful Professional Learning Communities at Work™ process.
Joint Publications With the International Reading Association
BKF578, BKF580, BKF582, BKF584, BKF586

Rebuilding the Foundation
Timothy V. Rasinski
Teaching reading is a complex task without a simple formula for developing quality instruction. Rather than build on or alter existing models, this book considers how educators and policymakers might think about rebuilding and reconceptualizing reading education, perhaps from the ground up.
BKF399

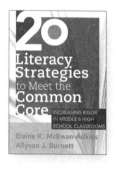

20 Literacy Strategies to Meet the Common Core
Elaine K. McEwan-Adkins and Allyson J. Burnett
With the advent of the Common Core State Standards, some secondary teachers are scrambling for what to do and how to do it. This book provides twenty research-based strategies designed to help students meet those standards and become expert readers.
BKF588

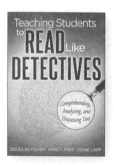

Teaching Students to Read Like Detectives
Douglas Fisher, Nancy Frey, and Diane Lapp
Prompt students to become the sophisticated readers, writers, and thinkers they need to be to achieve higher learning. Explore the important relationship between text, learner, and learning, and gain an array of methods to establish critical literacy in a discussion-based and reflective classroom.
BKF499

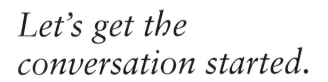